THE HEBREW ISRAELITE LAW BOOK

Our Laws, Statutes, Commandments, and Judgments

By Omar Mathis known as Yahudah Ben Yisrael

The Hebrew Israelite Law Book

Copyright © 2021 by Omar Mathis

The Hebrew Israelite Law Book

Table of Contents

Introduction 12

TITLE 1 – TREASON 1

Chapter 1-The Name of God 2

Chapter 2-Sedition and Subversive Activities............. 4

Chapter 3-Obedience 15

TITLE 2 – CALLING OF THE ASSEMBLY 39

TITLE 3 – FAMILY 43

Chapter 1-Husband 45

Chapter 2-Wife.. 46

Chapter 3-Son 48

Chapter 4-Daughter 51

Chapter 5-Adultery 52

Chapter 6-Elders 54

Chapter 7-Divorce 55

Chapter 8-A Jealous Husband 56

TITLE 4 – JUSTICE SYSTEM....................................61

Chapter 1-Judges... 62

Chapter 2-Court 64

Chapter 3-Witnesses 66

Chapter 4-Judgments 68

Chapter 5-Punishment.. 69

Chapter 6-Cities of Refuge for Murder 72

Chapter 7-King.. 75

TITLE 5 – NAKEDNESS...78

TITLE 6 – WHORISH ACTIONS 82

Chapter 1-Lying With...83

Chapter 2-Homosexuality..86

Chapter 3-Fornication 88

Chapter 4-Bestiality 89

Chapter 5-Whoring 91

Chapter 6-Nakedness...92

TITLE 7 – CRUELTY 96

Chapter 1-Mental Cruelty 97

Chapter 2-Verbal Cruelty..99

TITLE 8 – COVETOUSNESS.................................101

TITLE 9 - ASSAULT..104

TITLE 10 - THEFT 109

TITLE 11 - LIABILITY..112

TITLE 12 - MURDER..116

TITLE 13 – APPEARANCE.....................................120

TITLE 14 - STRANGERS 123

TITLE 15 – HELPING A BROTHER 126

TITLE 16 – TABERNACLE.....................................129

Chapter 1 – Offerings for the Tabernacle and Priesthood...133

Chapter 2 - Tabernacle Curtains..............................142

   A. Linen Tabernacle 143

   B. Goat Hair Covering 144

   C. Ram and Badger Skin Covering 146

   D. Hanging for the Door of the Tabernacle..........147

Chapter 3 - Tabernacle Boards 148

Chapter 4 - Bars for the Tabernacle Boards............ 151

Chapter 5 - Ark...153

Chapter 6 - Mercy Seat......................................155

Chapter 7 - Shewbread Table 157

Chapter 8 - Lamps.. 160

Chapter 9 - Vail 165

Chapter 10 – Altar of Earth...............................167

Chapter 11 – Altar of Shittim Wood...................... 168

Chapter 12 - Court of the Tabernacle...................... 171

TITLE 17 – LEVITES AND PRIESTHOOD.............176

Chapter 1 – Levites...177

   A. Separating the Levites..................................177

   B. The Tithe 180

   C. Heave Offering of the Tithe........................... 184

   D. Levite Inheritance.......................................185

Chapter 2 - Aaron and Sons as Priests.................... 188

   A. Defiled for the Dead 192

   B. Baldness 193

   C. Marriage 193

   D. Daughter 194

   E. Wine and Strong Drink 194

   F. Blemish...194

   G. Cleanliness 196

   H. Eating the Holy Things.................................197

   I. High Priest 198

      a. Uncovering His Head and Rending His Clothes 198

      b. Defile Himself and Leave the Sanctuary...... 198

c. Marriage 199

J. Aaron's Garment (High Priest) 199

a. Ephod 200

b. Girdle 202

c. Breastplate 202

d. Broidered Coat 205

e. Robe 207

f. Mitre 208

K. Aaron's Sons Garments (Priest's) 209

L. Hallowing the Priests 210

a. Bullock 212

b. Rams 213

c. Bread 215

d. Priest Seven Day Consecration 215

M. Incense Altar 217

N. Lavar of Brass for Washing the Priests Hands and Feet 220

O. Oil of Holy Ointment 221

P. Holy Perfume 222

Q. Aaron Given the Heave Offerings 223

TITLE 18 – OFFERINGS AND SACRIFICES 228

Chapter 1 – Sacrifice Preparation 229

Chapter 2 - First Fruits 234

A. Meat Offering 234

a. Fine Flour 235

b. Corn 235

Chapter 3 – Offering of Burnt Sacrifice 236

A. Herd 236

B. Flock 237

C. Fowls 238

Chapter 4 – Meat Offering (Baking) 239

A. Unbaked 239

B. Baked in an Oven 239

C. Baked in a Pan 240

D. Baked in a Fryingpan 240

E. Priest Presentation 240

Chapter 5 – Sacrifice of Peace Offering 242

A. Herd 242

B. Flock 243

a. Lamb 243

b. Goat 244

Chapter 6 – Sin Offering 246

A. If a Soul Sin Through Ignorance against any of the Commandments, If the Priest that is Anointed do Sin According to the Sin of the People 246

B. If the whole congregation of Israel sin through ignorance, and the thing is hid from the eyes of the assembly, and they have done somewhat against any of the commandments of the LORD concerning things which should be done and are guilty 248

C. A Ruler has Sinned and done somewhat through Ignorance any of the Commandments of the LORD his God concerning things which should not be done, and is guilty, Or if his sin, wherein he hath sinned, come to his knowledge 250

D. If any one of the Common People Sin through Ignorance, while he doeth somewhat against any of the Commandments of the LORD concerning things which ought not to be done, and be Guilty 251

a. Kid of the Goats 251

b. Female Lamb 252

Chapter 7 - Trespass Offering 254

A. Trespass Offering 1 254

a. Sin Offering..255

b. Sin and Burnt Offering 255

c. Sin and Meat Offering.................................. 256

B. Trespass Offering 2 256

C. Trespass Offering 3 257

D. Trespass Offering 4... 258

Chapter 8 – Law of the Burnt Offering.................. 260

Chapter 9 – Law of the Meat Offering 262

Chapter 10 - Offering when Aaron and his Sons are Anointed 264

Chapter 11 – Law of the Sin Offering..................... 266

Chapter 12 – Law of the Trespass Offering 268

Chapter 13 – Law of the Sacrifice of Peace Offerings 270

A. Thanksgiving Offering 270

B. Vow or Voluntary Offering................................271

Chapter 14 – When Israel first comes into the Land 276

A. Making Offerings 276

a. Flock...277

b. Herd... 278

B. When Israel first Eats the Bread of the Land . 278

C. If the Children of Israel Erred and Don't Keep Commandments...279

a. Sin through Ignorance Without the Knowledge of the Congregation 280

b. Sin Through Ignorance 280

c. Soul that Doeth Ought Presumptuously 281

D. Location of Sacrifices 281

E. First of All the Fruit of the Earth 286

Chapter 15 – Day by Day......................................288

Chapter 16 – On the Sabbath Day...........................290

Chapter 17 – In the Beginning of Every Month 291

TITLE 19 – CLEAN AND UNCLEAN....................... 293

Chapter 1-The Beast...296

Chapter 2-In the Waters 299

Chapter 3-Fowls.. 301

Chapter 4-Fowls that Creep 303

Chapter 5-The Creeping Things 305

Chapter 6-Woman that has Conceived 308

A. A Man Child 308

B. A Maid Child 308

C. Burnt Offering 309

Chapter 7-Leprosy... 311

A. On the Skin.. 311

B. On the Head or Beard 315

C. In the Garment...317

D. In the Day of His Cleansing 320

E. In the House... 324

Chapter 8-Running Issue.......................................328

A. Out of the Flesh 328

B. A Man's Seed 330

C. A Woman's issue of Blood................................331

Chapter 9-Water of Separation: A Purification for Sin 334

TITLE 20 – NAZARITE VOW 339

TITLE 21 – HOLY CONVOCATIONS 345

Chapter 1-Passover 1 346

Chapter 2-Passover 2 351

Chapter 3-Feast of Unleavened Bread 354

Chapter 4-Sabbath 357

Chapter 5-Feast of Harvest 361

Chapter 6-Blowing of Trumpets 365

Chapter 7-Day of Atonement 366

Chapter 8-Feast of Tabernacles 374

TITLE 22 – MALE APPEARANCE 382

TITLE 23 - COMMERCIAL ACTIVITIES 384

Chapter 1-Weights 385

Chapter 2-Loans 387

Chapter 3-Labor 389

Chapter 4-Agriculture 395

Chapter 5-The Jubilee 401

Chapter 6-The Poor 403

Chapter 7-Land and Property 406

Chapter 8-Release 411

TITLE 24 – WARFARE 413

TITLE 25 – ISRAELITE NUMBERING 424

TITLE 26 – SINGULAR VOWS AND SANCTIFYING 431

Chapter 1-Shekel Payment 432

Chapter 2-Beasts 433

Chapter 3-Sanctify His House..................................435

Chapter 4-Sanctifying Fields.....................................436

Chapter 5-Men and Women who make a Vow 438

TITLE 27 - INHERITANCE 443

TITLE 28 – PROPHET 448

TITLE 29 – ENTERING INTO THE CONGREGATION
....450

TITLE 30 – CIRCUMCISION 454

The Hebrew Israelite Law Book

Introduction

Our Chief Elder said, "we would be surprised how many people don't know the ten commandments." Instantly I felt ashamed. I was one of those people. At that moment, I promised myself that I would learn them. The next day, sitting down on my living room floor, I started studying them. While doing that, I said to myself, "If I'm an Israelite, I should know all of the law." So, I went to the store and purchased a three-ring binder, notebook paper, and dividers. I sat down on my living room floor and wrote each law on its own sheet of paper and put them in sections for each subject. That binder went through several improvements to finally become this book.

I hoped selling a book would not be necessary. Well, here am I. Absorbing the reality of what it takes to be free and writing this book to those true zealots for freedom. The only way for our people to be free is through the laws, statutes, commandments, and judgments. The problem is most people have their own beliefs and feelings about what is righteous. So, there is always somethings they will reject. I've had Hebrew Israelites curse the law and hate me for just reading the law in a peaceful manner. I realized early on that this is the price that must be paid. It has always been this way.

I've published this book is to make the laws, statutes, commandments, and judgments easy to find. I will continue to publish other books containing the law to bring understanding to our culture.

Please take advantage of the blank pages to write down any notes.

Also, this book is not about Judaism, Rabbinical Law, Talmud, or any of the other religions. It is about Hebrew Israelite culture and government.

www.hebrewisraeltelaw.org.

The Hebrew Israelite Law Book

The Hebrew Israelite Law Book

TITLE 1 – TREASON

Chapter 1-The Name of God

Leviticus 19

12 And ye shall not swear by my name falsely, neither shalt thou profane the name of thy God: I am the Lord.

Leviticus 22

32 Neither shall ye profane my holy name; but I will be hallowed among the children of Israel: I am the LORD which hallow you,

33 That brought you out of the land of Egypt, to be your God: I am the LORD.

Leviticus 24

15 And thou shalt speak unto the children of Israel, saying, Whosoever curseth his God shall bear his sin.

16 And he that blasphemeth the name of the LORD, he shall surely be put to death, and all the congregation shall certainly stone him: as well the stranger, as he that is born in the land, when he blasphemeth the name of the Lord, shall be put to death.

Numbers 6

22 And the LORD spake unto Moses, saying,

23 Speak unto Aaron and unto his sons, saying, On this wise ye shall bless the children of Israel, saying unto them,

24 The LORD bless thee, and keep thee:

25 The Lord make his face shine upon thee, and be gracious unto thee:

26 The Lord lift up his countenance upon thee, and give thee peace.

27 And they shall put my name upon the children of Israel; and I will bless them.

Deuteronomy 6

13 Thou shalt fear the Lord thy God, and serve him, and shalt swear by his name.

Chapter 2-Sedition and Subversive Activities

Exodus 20

2   I am the LORD thy God, which have brought thee out of the land of Egypt, out of the house of bondage.

3   Thou shalt have no other gods before me.

4   Thou shalt not make unto thee any graven image, or any likeness of any thing that is in heaven above, or that is in the earth beneath, or that is in the water under the earth:

5   Thou shalt not bow down thyself to them, nor serve them: for I the LORD thy God am a jealous God, visiting the iniquity of the fathers upon the children unto the third and fourth generation of them that hate me;

6   And shewing mercy unto thousands of them that love me, and keep my commandments.

Exodus 20

7   Thou shalt not take the name of the LORD thy God in vain; for the LORD will not hold him guiltless that taketh his name in vain.

Exodus 20
22   And the LORD said unto Moses, Thus thou shalt say unto the children of Israel, Ye have seen that I have talked with you from heaven.
23   Ye shall not make with me gods of silver, neither shall ye make unto you gods of gold.

Exodus 22
18   Thou shalt not suffer a witch to live.

Exodus 22
20   He that sacrificeth unto any god, save unto the LORD only, he shall be utterly destroyed.

Exodus 23
13   And in all things that I have said unto you be circumspect: and make no mention of the name of other gods, neither let it be heard out of thy mouth.

Exodus 34
17   Thou shalt make thee no molten gods.

Leviticus 18

21 And thou shalt not let any of thy seed pass through the fire to Molech, neither shalt thou profane the name of thy God: I am the Lord.

Leviticus 19

4 Turn ye not unto idols, nor make to yourselves molten gods: I am the Lord your God.

Leviticus 19

31 Regard not them that have familiar spirits, neither seek after wizards, to be defiled by them: I am the LORD your God.

Leviticus 20

1 And the Lord spake unto Moses, saying,

2 Again, thou shalt say to the children of Israel, Whosoever he be of the children of Israel, or of the strangers that sojourn in Israel, that giveth any of his seed unto Molech; he shall surely be put to death: the people of the land shall stone him with stones.

3 And I will set my face against that man, and will cut him off from among his people; because he hath given of his seed unto

Molech, to defile my sanctuary, and to profane my holy name.

4   And if the people of the land do any ways hide their eyes from the man, when he giveth of his seed unto Molech, and kill him not:

5   Then I will set my face against that man, and against his family, and will cut him off, and all that go a whoring after him, to commit whoredom

with Molech, from among their people.

6   And the soul that turneth after such as have familiar spirits, and after wizards, to go a whoring after them, I will even set my face against that soul, and will cut him off from among his people.

7   Sanctify yourselves therefore, and be ye holy: for I am the LORD your God.

8   And ye shall keep my statutes, and do them: I am the LORD which sanctify you.

Leviticus 20
27 A man also or woman that hath a familiar spirit, or that is a wizard, shall surely be put to death: they shall stone them with stones: their blood shall be upon them.

Leviticus 26
1   Ye shall make you no idols nor graven image, neither rear you up a standing image,

neither shall ye set up any image of stone in your land

2   Ye shall keep my sabbaths, and reverence my sanctuary: I am the LORD.

Deuteronomy 5

7   Thou shalt have none other gods before me.

8   Thou shalt not make thee any graven image, or any likeness of any thing that is in heaven above, or that is in the earth beneath, or that is in the waters beneath the earth:

9   Thou shalt not bow down thyself unto them, nor serve them: for I the Lord thy God am a jealous God, visiting the iniquity of the fathers upon the children unto the third and fourth generation of them that hate me,

10   And shewing mercy unto thousands of them that love me and keep my commandments.

11   Thou shalt not take the name of the Lord thy God in vain: for the Lord will not hold him guiltless that taketh his name in vain.

Deuteronomy 6

14   Ye shall not go after other gods, of the gods of the people which are round about you;

15   (For the Lord thy God is a jealous God among you) lest the anger of the Lord thy God

be kindled against thee, and destroy thee from off the face of the earth.

16 Ye shall not tempt the Lord your God, as ye tempted him in Massah.

Deuteronomy 12

29 When the LORD thy God shall cut off the nations from before thee, whither thou goest to possess them, and thou suceedest them, and dwellest in their land;

30 Take heed to thyself that thou be not snared by following them, after that they be destroyed from before thee; and that thou inquire not after their gods, saying, How did these nations serve their gods? even so will I do likewise.

31 Thou shalt not do so unto the LORD thy God: for every abomination to the LORD, which he hateth, have they done unto their gods; for even their sons and their daughters they have burnt in the fire to their gods.

32 What thing soever I command you, observe to do it: thou shalt not add thereto, nor diminish from it.

Deuteronomy 13

1 If there arise among you a prophet, or a dreamer of dreams, and giveth thee a sign or a wonder,

2   And the sign or the wonder come to pass, whereof he spake unto thee, saying, Let us go after other gods, which thou hast not known, and let us serve them;

3   Thou shalt not hearken unto the words of that prophet, or that dreamer of dreams: for the LORD your God proveth you, to know whether ye love the LORD your God with all your heart and with all your soul.

4   Ye shall walk after the LORD your God, and fear him, and keep his commandments, and obey his voice, and ye shall serve him, and cleave unto him.

5   And that prophet, or that dreamer of dreams, shall be put to death; because he hath spoken to turn you away from the LORD your God, which brought you out of the land of Egypt, and redeemed you out of the house of bondage, to thrust thee out of the way which the LORD thy God commanded thee to walk in. So shalt thou put the evil away from the midst of thee.

Deuteronomy 13
6   If thy brother, the son of thy mother, or thy son, or thy daughter, or the wife of thy bosom, or thy friend, which is as thine own soul, entice thee secretly, saying, Let us go and serve other gods, which thou hast not known, thou, nor thy fathers;

7   Namely, of the gods of the people which are round about you, nigh unto thee, or far off from thee, from the one end of the earth even unto the other end of the earth;

8   Thou shalt not consent unto him, nor hearken unto him; neither shall thine eye pity him, neither shalt thou spare, neither shalt thou conceal him:

9   But thou shalt surely kill him; thine hand shall be first upon him to put him to death, and afterwards the hand of all the people.

10   And thou shalt stone him with stones, that he die; because he hath sought to thrust thee away from the LORD thy God, which brought thee out of the land of Egypt, from the house of bondage.

11   And all Israel shall hear, and fear, and shall do no more any such wickedness as this is among you.

Deuteronomy 13

12   If thou shalt hear say in one of thy cities, which the LORD thy God hath given thee to dwell there, saying,

13   Certain men, the children of Belial, are gone out from among you, and have withdrawn the inhabitants of their city, saying, Let us go and serve other gods, which ye have not known;

14 Then shalt thou inquire, and make search, and ask diligently; and, behold, if it be truth, and the thing certain, that such abomination is wrought

among you;

15 Thou shalt surely smite the inhabitants of that city with the edge of the sword, destroying it utterly, and all that is therein, and the cattle thereof, with the edge of the sword.

16 And thou shalt gather all the spoil of it into the midst of the street thereof, and shalt burn with fire the city, and all the spoil thereof every whit, for the LORD thy God: and it shall be an heap for ever; it shall

not be built again.

17 And there shall cleave nought of the cursed thing to thine hand: that the LORD may turn from the fierceness of his anger, and shew thee mercy, and have compassion upon thee, and multiply thee, as he hath sworn

unto thy fathers;

18 When thou shalt hearken to the voice of the LORD thy God, to keep all his commandments which I command thee this day, to do that which is

right in the eyes of the LORD thy God.

Deuteronomy 16

21 Thou shalt not plant thee a grove of any trees near unto the altar of the LORD thy God, which thou shalt make thee.

22 Neither shalt thou set thee up any image; which the Lord thy God hateth.

Deuteronomy 17

2 If there be found among you, within any of thy gates which the LORD thy God giveth thee, man or woman, that hath wrought wickedness in the sight of the LORD thy God, in transgressing his covenant,

3 And hath gone and served other gods, and worshipped them, either the sun, or moon, or any of the host of heaven, which I have not commanded;

4 And it be told thee, and thou hast heard of it, and inquired diligently, and, behold, it be true, and the thing certain, that such abomination is wrought in Israel:

5 Then shalt thou bring forth that man or that woman, which have committed that wicked thing, unto thy gates, even that man or that woman, and shalt stone them with stones, till they die.

6 At the mouth of two witnesses, or three witnesses, shall he that is worthy of death be put to death; but at the mouth of one witness he shall not be put to death.

7   The hands of the witnesses shall be first upon him to put him to death, and afterward the hands of all the people. So thou shalt put the evil away from among you.

Deuteronomy 18

10   There shall not be found among you any one that maketh his son or his daughter to pass through the fire, or that useth divination, or an observer of times, or an enchanter, or a witch,

11   Or a charmer, or a consulter with familiar spirits, or a wizard, or a necromancer.

12   For all that do these things are an abomination unto the LORD: and because of these abominations the LORD thy God doth drive them out from before thee.

13   Thou shalt be perfect with the LORD thy God.

14   For these nations, which thou shalt possess, hearkened unto observers of times, and unto diviners: but as for thee, the LORD thy God hath not suffered thee so to do

Chapter 3-Obedience

Exodus 19

3   And Moses went up unto God, and the LORD called unto him out of the mountain, saying, Thus shalt thou say to the house of Jacob, and tell the children of Israel;

4 Ye have seen what I did unto the Egyptians, and how I bare you on eagles' wings, and brought you unto myself.

5   Now therefore, if ye will obey my voice indeed, and keep my covenant, then ye shall be a peculiar treasure unto me above all people: for all the earth is mine:

6   And ye shall be unto me a kingdom of priests, and an holy nation. These are the words which thou shalt speak unto the children of Israel.

7   And Moses came and called for the elders of the people, and laid before their faces all these words which the Lord commanded him.

8   And all the people answered together, and said, All that the LORD hath spoken we will do. And Moses returned the words of the people unto the LORD.

Leviticus 18

1   And the Lord spake unto Moses, saying,

2   Speak unto the children of Israel, and say unto them, I am the LORD your God.

3   After the doings of the land of Egypt, wherein ye dwelt, shall ye not do: and after the doings of the land of Canaan, whither I bring you, shall ye not do: neither shall ye walk in their ordinances.

4   Ye shall do my judgments, and keep mine ordinances, to walk therein: I am the Lord your God.

5   Ye shall therefore keep my statutes, and my judgments: which if a man do, he shall live in them: I am the Lord.

Leviticus 19

1   And the LORD spake unto Moses, saying,

2   Speak unto all the congregation of the children of Israel, and say unto them, Ye shall be holy: for I the Lord your God am holy.

Leviticus 20

22 Ye shall therefore keep all my statutes, and all my judgments, and do them: that the land, whither I bring you to dwell therein, spue you not out.

23 And ye shall not walk in the manners of the nation, which I cast out before you: for they committed all these things, and therefore I abhorred them.

24 But I have said unto you, Ye shall inherit their land, and I will give it unto you to possess it, a land that floweth with milk and honey: I am the LORD your God, which have separated you from other people.

25 Ye shall therefore put difference between clean beasts and unclean, and between unclean fowls and clean: and ye shall not make your souls abominable by beast, or by fowl, or by any manner of living thing that creepeth on the ground, which I have separated from you as unclean.

26 And ye shall be holy unto me: for I the LORD am holy, and have severed you from other people, that ye should be mine.

Leviticus 26

3 If ye walk in my statutes, and keep my commandments, and do them;

4 Then I will give you rain in due season, and the land shall yield her increase, and the trees of the field shall yield their fruit.

5 And your threshing shall reach unto the vintage, and the vintage shall reach unto the sowing time: and ye shall eat your bread to the full, and dwell in your land safely.

6   And I will give peace in the land, and ye shall lie down, and none shall make you afraid: and I will rid evil beasts out of the land, neither shall the sword go through your land.

7   And ye shall chase your enemies, and they shall fall before you by the sword.

8   And five of you shall chase an hundred, and an hundred of you shall put ten thousand to flight: and your enemies shall fall before you by the sword.

9   For I will have respect unto you, and make you fruitful, and multiply you, and establish my covenant with you.

10   And ye shall eat old store, and bring forth the old because of the new.

11   And I will set my tabernacle among you: and my soul shall not abhor you.

12   And I will walk among you, and will be your God, and ye shall be my people.

13   I am the LORD your God, which brought you forth out of the land of Egypt, that ye should not be their bondmen; and I have broken the bands of your yoke, and made you go upright.

Leviticus 26

14   But if ye will not hearken unto me, and will not do all these commandments;

15   And if ye shall despise my statutes, or if your soul abhor my judgments, so that ye will not do all my commandments, but that ye break my covenant:

16   I also will do this unto you; I will even appoint over you terror, consumption, and the burning ague, that shall consume the eyes, and cause sorrow of heart: and ye shall sow your seed in vain, for your enemies shall eat it.

17   And I will set my face against you, and ye shall be slain before your enemies: they that hate you shall reign over you; and ye shall flee when none pursueth you.

18   And if ye will not yet for all this hearken unto me, then I will punish you seven times more for your sins.

19   And I will break the pride of your power; and I will make your heaven as iron, and your earth as brass:

20   And your strength shall be spent in vain: for your land shall not yield her increase, neither shall the trees of the land yield their fruits.

21   And if ye walk contrary unto me, and will not hearken unto me; I will bring seven times more plagues upon you according to your sins.

22   I will also send wild beasts among you, which shall rob you of your children, and

destroy your cattle, and make you few in number; and your high ways shall be desolate.

23 And if ye will not be reformed by me by these things, but will walk contrary unto me;

24 Then will I also walk contrary unto you, and will punish you yet seven times for your sins.

25 And I will bring a sword upon you, that shall avenge the quarrel of my covenant: and when ye are gathered together within your cities, I will send the pestilence among you; and ye shall be delivered into the hand of the enemy.

26 And when I have broken the staff of your bread, ten women shall bake your bread in one oven, and they shall deliver you your bread again by weight: and ye shall eat, and not be satisfied.

27 And if ye will not for all this hearken unto me, but walk contrary unto me;

28 Then I will walk contrary unto you also in fury; and I, even I, will chastise you seven times for your sins.

29 And ye shall eat the flesh of your sons, and the flesh of your daughters shall ye eat.

30 And I will destroy your high places, and cut down your images, and cast your carcases upon the carcases of your idols, and my soul shall abhor you.

31 And I will make your cities waste, and bring your sanctuaries unto desolation, and I will not smell the savour of your sweet odours.

32 And I will bring the land into desolation: and your enemies which dwell therein shall be astonished at it.

33 And I will scatter you among the heathen, and will draw out a sword after you: and your land shall be desolate, and your cities waste.

34 Then shall the land enjoy her sabbaths, as long as it lieth desolate, and ye be in your enemies' land; even then shall the land rest, and enjoy her sabbaths.

35 As long as it lieth desolate it shall rest; because it did not rest in your sabbaths, when ye dwelt upon it.

36 And upon them that are left alive of you I will send a faintness into their hearts in the lands of their enemies; and the sound of a shaken leaf shall chase them; and they shall flee, as fleeing from a sword; and they shall fall when none pursueth.

37 And they shall fall one upon another, as it were before a sword, when none pursueth: and ye shall have no power to stand before your enemies.

38 And ye shall perish among the heathen, and the land of your enemies shall eat you up.

39 And they that are left of you shall pine away in their iniquity in your enemies' lands; and also in the iniquities of their fathers shall they pine away with them.

40 If they shall confess their iniquity, and the iniquity of their fathers, with their trespass which they trespassed against me, and that also they have walked contrary unto me;

41 And that I also have walked contrary unto them, and have brought them into the land of their enemies; if then their uncircumcised hearts be humbled, and they then accept of the punishment of their iniquity:

42 Then will I remember my covenant with Jacob, and also my covenant with Isaac, and also my covenant with Abraham will I remember; and I will remember the land.

43 The land also shall be left of them, and shall enjoy her sabbaths, while she lieth desolate without them: and they shall accept of the punishment of their iniquity: because, even because they despised my judgments, and because their soul abhorred my statutes.

44 And yet for all that, when they be in the land of their enemies, I will not cast them away, neither will I abhor them, to destroy them utterly, and to break my covenant with them: for I am the LORD their God.

45 But I will for their sakes remember the covenant of their ancestors, whom I brought forth out of the land of Egypt in the sight of the heathen, that I might be their God: I am the LORD.

46 These are the statutes and judgments and laws, which the LORD made between him and the children of Israel in mount Sinai by the hand of Moses.

Deuteronomy 4

5   Behold, I have taught you statutes and judgments, even as the LORD my God commanded me, that ye should do so in the land whither ye go to possess it.

6   Keep therefore and do them; for this is your wisdom and your understanding in the sight of the nations, which shall hear all these statutes, and say, Surely this great nation is a wise and understanding people.

7   For what nation is there so great, who hath God so nigh unto them, as the Lord our God is in all things that we call upon him for?

8   And what nation is there so great, that hath statutes and judgments so righteous as all this law, which I set before you this day?

9   Only take heed to thyself, and keep thy soul diligently, lest thou forget the things which thine eyes have seen, and lest they

depart from thy heart all the days of thy life: but teach them thy sons, and thy sons' sons;

10 Specially the day that thou stoodest before the Lord thy God in Horeb, when the Lord said unto me, Gather me the people together, and I will make them hear my words, that they may learn to fear me all the days that they shall live upon the earth, and that they may teach their children.

11 And ye came near and stood under the mountain; and the mountain burned with fire unto the midst of heaven, with darkness, clouds, and thick darkness.

12 And the Lord spake unto you out of the midst of the fire: ye heard the voice of the words, but saw no similitude; only ye heard a voice.

13 And he declared unto you his covenant, which he commanded you to perform, even ten commandments; and he wrote them upon two tables of stone.

14 And the LORD commanded me at that time to teach you statutes and judgments, that ye might do them in the land whither ye go over to possess it.

15 Take ye therefore good heed unto yourselves; for ye saw no manner of similitude on the day that the Lord spake unto you in Horeb out of the midst of the fire:

16 Lest ye corrupt yourselves, and make you a graven image, the similitude of any figure, the likeness of male or female,

17 The likeness of any beast that is on the earth, the likeness of any winged fowl that flieth in the air,

18 The likeness of any thing that creepeth on the ground, the likeness of any fish that is in the waters beneath the earth:

19 And lest thou lift up thine eyes unto heaven, and when thou seest the sun, and the moon, and the stars, even all the host of heaven, shouldest be driven to worship them, and serve them, which the Lord thy God hath divided unto all nations under the whole heaven.

Deuteronomy 5

1 And Moses called all Israel, and said unto them, Hear, O Israel, the statutes and judgments which I speak in your ears this day, that ye may learn them, and keep, and do them.

2 The LORD our God made a covenant with us in Horeb.

3 The Lord made not this covenant with our fathers, but with us, even us, who are all of us here alive this day.

4 The LORD talked with you face to face in the mount out of the midst of the fire,

5   (I stood between the LORD and you at that time, to shew you the word of the LORD: for ye were afraid by reason of the fire, and went not up into the mount;) saying,

6   I am the Lord thy God, which brought thee out of the land of Egypt, from the house of bondage.

Deuteronomy 6

1   Now these are the commandments, the statutes, and the judgments, which the Lord your God commanded to teach you, that ye might do them in the land whither ye go to possess it:

2   That thou mightest fear the LORD thy God, to keep all his statutes and his commandments, which I command thee, thou, and thy son, and thy son's son, all the days of thy life; and that thy days may be prolonged.

3   Hear therefore, O Israel, and observe to do it; that it may be well with thee, and that ye may increase mightily, as the Lord God of thy fathers hath promised thee, in the land that floweth with milk and honey.

4   Hear, O Israel: The Lord our God is one Lord:

5   And thou shalt love the LORD thy God with all thine heart, and with all thy soul, and with all thy might.

6   And these words, which I command thee this day, shall be in thine heart:

7   And thou shalt teach them diligently unto thy children, and shalt talk of them when thou sittest in thine house, and when thou walkest by the way, and when thou liest down, and when thou risest up.

8   And thou shalt bind them for a sign upon thine hand, and they shall be as frontlets between thine eyes.

9   And thou shalt write them upon the posts of thy house, and on thy gates.

10   And it shall be, when the Lord thy God shall have brought thee into the land which he sware unto thy fathers, to Abraham, to Isaac, and to Jacob, to give thee great and goodly cities, which thou buildedst not,

11   And houses full of all good things, which thou filledst not, and wells digged, which thou diggedst not, vineyards and olive trees, which thou plantedst not; when thou shalt have eaten and be full;

12   Then beware lest thou forget the Lord, which brought thee forth out of the land of Egypt, from the house of bondage.

Deuteronomy 6
17 Ye   shall   diligently   keep   the commandments of the Lord your God, and

his testimonies, and his statutes, which he hath commanded thee.

18 And thou shalt do that which is right and good in the sight of the LORD: that it may be well with thee, and that thou mayest go in and possess the good land which the Lord sware unto thy fathers,

19 To cast out all thine enemies from before thee, as the LORD hath spoken.

20 And when thy son asketh thee in time to come, saying,

What mean the testimonies, and the statutes, and the judgments, which the LORD our God hath commanded you?

21 Then thou shalt say unto thy son, We were Pharaoh's bondmen in Egypt; and the LORD brought us out of Egypt with a mighty hand:

22 And the LORD shewed signs and wonders, great and sore, upon Egypt, upon Pharaoh, and upon all his household, before our eyes:

23 And he brought us out from thence, that he might bring us in, to give us the land which he sware unto our fathers.

24 And the LORD commanded us to do all these statutes, to fear the LORD our God, for our good always, that he might preserve us alive, as it is at this day.

25 And it shall be our righteousness, if we observe to do all these commandments before the LORD our God, as he hath commanded us.

Deuteronomy 7

9 Know therefore that the LORD thy God, he is God, the faithful God, which keepeth covenant and mercy with them that love him and keep his commandments to a thousand generations;

10 And repayeth them that hate him to their face, to destroy them: he will not be slack to him that hateth him, he will repay him to his face.

11 Thou shalt therefore keep the commandments, and the statutes, and the judgments, which I command thee this day, to do them.

12 Wherefore it shall come to pass, if ye hearken to these judgments, and keep, and do them, that the LORD thy God shall keep unto thee the covenant and the mercy which he sware unto thy fathers:

13 And he will love thee, and bless thee, and multiply thee: he will also bless the fruit of thy womb, and the fruit of thy land, thy corn, and thy wine, and thine oil, the increase of thy kine, and the flocks of thy sheep, in the

land which he sware unto thy fathers to give thee.

14   Thou shalt be blessed above all people: there shall not be male or female barren among you, or among your cattle.

15   And the LORD will take away from thee all sickness, and will put none of the evil diseases of Egypt, which thou knowest, upon thee; but will lay them upon all them that hate thee.

16   And thou shalt consume all the people which the LORD thy God shall deliver thee; thine eye shall have no pity upon them: neither shalt thou serve their gods; for that will be a snare unto thee.

17   If thou shalt say in thine heart, These nations are more than I; how can I dispossess them?

18   Thou shalt not be afraid of them: but shalt well remember what the LORD thy God did unto Pharaoh, and unto all Egypt;

19   The great temptations which thine eyes saw, and the signs, and the wonders, and the mighty hand, and the stretched out arm, whereby the LORD thy God brought thee out: so shall the LORD thy God do unto all the people of whom thou art afraid.

20   Moreover the LORD thy God will send the hornet among them, until they that are

left, and hide themselves from thee, be destroyed.

21 Thou shalt not be affrighted at them: for the LORD thy God is among you, a mighty God and terrible.

22 And the LORD thy God will put out those nations before thee by little and little: thou mayest not consume them at once, lest the beasts of the field increase upon thee.

23 But the LORD thy God shall deliver them unto thee, and shall destroy them with a mighty destruction, until they be destroyed.

24 And he shall deliver their kings into thine hand, and thou shalt destroy their name from under heaven: there shall no man be able to stand before thee, until thou have destroyed them.

25 The graven images of their gods shall ye burn with fire: thou shalt not desire the silver or gold that is on them, nor take it unto thee, lest thou be snared therein: for it is an abomination to the LORD thy God.

26 Neither shalt thou bring an abomination into thine house, lest thou be a cursed thing like it: but thou shalt utterly detest it, and thou shalt utterly abhor it; for it is a cursed thing.

Deuteronomy 8

1　All the commandments which I command thee this day shall ye observe to do, that ye may live, and multiply, and go in and possess the land which the LORD sware unto your fathers.

2　And thou shalt remember all the way which the LORD thy God led thee these forty years in the wilderness, to humble thee, and to prove thee, to know what was in thine heart, whether thou wouldest keep his commandments, or no.

3　And he humbled thee, and suffered thee to hunger, and fed thee with manna, which thou knewest not, neither did thy fathers know; that he might make thee know that man doth not live by bread only, but by every word that proceedeth out of the mouth of the LORD doth man live.

4　Thy raiment waxed not old upon thee, neither did thy foot swell, these forty years.

5　Thou shalt also consider in thine heart, that, as a man chasteneth his son, so the LORD thy God chasteneth thee.

6　Therefore thou shalt keep the commandments of the LORD thy God, to walk in his ways, and to fear him.

Deuteronomy 10

12　And now, Israel, what doth the LORD thy God require of thee, but to fear the LORD thy God, to walk in all his ways, and to love him, and to serve the LORD thy God with all thy heart and with all thy soul,

13 To keep the commandments of the LORD, and his statutes, which I command thee this day for thy good?

14 Behold, the heaven and the heaven of heavens is the LORD'S thy God, the earth also, with all that therein is.

15 Only the LORD had a delight in thy fathers to love them, and he chose their seed after them, even you above all people, as it is this day.

16 Circumcise therefore the foreskin of your heart, and be no more stiffnecked.

17 For the LORD your God is God of gods, and Lord of lords, a great God, a mighty, and a terrible, which regardeth not persons, nor taketh reward:

18 He doth execute the judgment of the fatherless and widow, and loveth the stranger, in giving him food and raiment.

19 Love ye therefore the stranger: for ye were strangers in the land of Egypt.

20 Thou shalt fear the LORD thy God; him shalt thou serve, and to him shalt thou cleave, and swear by his name.

21 He is thy praise, and he is thy God, that hath done for thee these great and terrible things, which thine eyes have seen.

22 Thy fathers went down into Egypt with threescore and ten persons; and now the LORD thy God hath made thee as the stars of heaven for multitude.

Deuteronomy 11

1 Therefore thou shalt love the LORD thy God, and keep his charge, and his statutes, and his judgments, and his commandments, always.

2 And know ye this day: for I speak not with your children which have not known, and which have not seen the chastisement of the LORD your God, his greatness, his mighty hand, and his stretched out arm,

3 And his miracles, and his acts, which he did in the midst of Egypt unto Pharaoh the king of Egypt, and unto all his land;

4 And what he did unto the army of Egypt, unto their horses, and to their chariots; how he made the water of the Red sea to overflow them as they pursued after you, and how the LORD hath destroyed them unto this day;

5 And what he did unto you in the wilderness, until ye came into this place;

6 And what he did unto Dathan and Abiram, the sons of Eliab, the son of Reuben: how the earth opened her mouth, and swallowed them up, and their households,

and their tents, and all the substance that was in their possession, in the midst of all Israel:

7   But your eyes have seen all the great acts of the LORD which he did.

8   Therefore shall ye keep all the commandments which I command you this day, that ye may be strong, and go in and possess the land, whither ye go to possess it;

9   And that ye may prolong your days in the land, which the LORD sware unto your fathers to give unto them and to their seed, a land that floweth with milk and honey.

10   For the land, whither thou goest in to possess it, is not as the land of Egypt, from whence ye came out, where thou so whence thy seed, and wateredst it with thy foot, as a garden of herbs:

11   But the land, whither ye go to possess it, is a land of hills and valleys, and drinketh water of the rain of heaven:

12   A land which the Lord thy God careth for: the eyes of the Lord thy God are always upon it, from the beginning of the year even unto the end of the year.

13   And it shall come to pass, if ye shall hearken diligently unto my commandments which I command you this day, to love the LORD your God, and to serve him with all your heart and with all your soul,

14 That I will give you the rain of your land in his due season, the first rain and the latter rain, that thou mayest gather in thy corn, and thy wine, and thine oil.

15 And I will send grass in thy fields for thy cattle, that thou mayest eat and be full.

16 Take heed to yourselves, that your heart be not deceived, and ye turn aside, and serve other gods, and worship them;

17 And then the LORD'S wrath be kindled against you, and he shut up the heaven, that there be no rain, and that the land yield not her fruit; and lest ye perish quickly from off the good land which the LORD giveth you.

18 Therefore shall ye lay up these my words in your heart and in your soul, and bind them for a sign upon your hand, that they may be as frontlets between your eyes.

19 And ye shall teach them your children, speaking of them when thou sittest in thine house, and when thou walkest by the way, when thou liest down, and when thou risest up.

20 And thou shalt write them upon the door posts of thine house, and upon thy gates:

21 That your days may be multiplied, and the days of your children, in the land which the LORD sware unto your fathers to give them, as the days of heaven upon the earth.

22 For if ye shall diligently keep all these commandments which I command you, to do them, to love the LORD your God, to walk in all his ways, and to cleave unto him;

23 Then will the LORD drive out all these nations from before you, and ye shall possess greater nations and mightier than yourselves.

24 Every place whereon the soles of your feet shall tread shall be yours: from the wilderness and Lebanon, from the river, the river Euphrates, even unto the uttermost sea shall your coast be.

25 There shall no man be able to stand before you: for the LORD your God shall lay the fear of you and the dread of you upon all the land that ye shall tread upon, as he hath said unto you.

26 Behold, I set before you this day a blessing and a curse;

27 A blessing, if ye obey the commandments of the LORD your God, which I command you this day:

28 And a curse, if ye will not obey the commandments of the LORD your God, but turn aside out of the way which I command you this day, to go after other gods, which ye have not known.

29 And it shall come to pass, when the LORD thy God hath brought thee in unto the land whither thou goest to possess it, that

thou shalt put the blessing upon mount Gerizim, and the curse upon mount Ebal.

30 Are they not on the other side Jordan, by the way where the sun goeth down, in the land of the Canaanites, which dwell in the champaign over against Gilgal, beside the plains of Moreh?

31 For ye shall pass over Jordan to go in to possess the land which the LORD your God giveth you, and ye shall possess it, and dwell therein.

32 And ye shall observe to do all the statutes and judgments which I set before you this day.

TITLE 2 – CALLING OF THE ASSEMBLY

Numbers 10

1   And the LORD spake unto Moses, saying,

2   Make thee two trumpets of silver; of a whole piece shalt thou make them: that thou mayest use them for the calling of the assembly, and for the journeying of the camps.

3   And when they shall blow with them, all the assembly shall assemble themselves to thee at the door of the tabernacle of the congregation.

4   And if they blow but with one trumpet, then the princes, which are heads of the thousands of Israel, shall gather themselves unto thee.

5   When ye blow an alarm, then the camps that lie on the east parts shall go forward.

6   When ye blow an alarm the second time, then the camps that lie on the south side

shall take their journey: they shall blow an alarm for their journeys.

7   But when the congregation is to be gathered together, ye shall blow, but ye shall not sound an alarm.

8   And the sons of Aaron, the priests, shall blow with the trumpets; and they shall be to you for an ordinance for ever throughout your generations.

9   And if ye go to war in your land against the enemy that oppresseth you, then ye shall blow an alarm with the trumpets; and ye shall be remembered before the LORD your God, and ye shall be saved from your enemies.

10   Also in the day of your gladness, and in your solemn days, and in the beginnings of your months, ye shall blow with the trumpets over your burnt offerings, and over the sacrifices of your peace offerings; that they may be to you for a memorial before your God: I am the LORD your God.

The Hebrew Israelite Law Book

The Hebrew Israelite Law Book

TITLE 3 – FAMILY

Exodus 20

12 Honour thy father and thy mother: that thy days may be long upon the land which the LORD thy God giveth thee.

Leviticus 19

3   Ye shall fear every man his mother, and his father, and keep my sabbaths: I am the Lord your God.

Leviticus 20

9   For every one that curseth his father or his mother shall be surely put to death: he hath cursed his father or his mother; his blood shall be upon him.

Deuteronomy 5

16 Honour thy father and thy mother, as the LORD thy God hath commanded thee; that thy days may be prolonged, and that it may go well with thee, in the land which the LORD thy God giveth thee.

The Hebrew Israelite Law Book

Chapter 1-Husband

Deuteronomy 24

6   When a man hath taken a new wife, he shall not go out to war, neither shall he be charged with any business: but he shall be free at home one year, and shall cheer up his wife which he hath taken.

Chapter 2-Wife

Deuteronomy 22

13   If any man take a wife, and go in unto her, and hate her,

14   And give occasions of speech against her, and bring up an evil name upon her, and say, I took this woman, and when I came to her, I found her not a maid:

15   Then shall the father of the damsel, and her mother, take and bring forth the tokens of the damsel's virginity unto the elders of the city in the gate:

16   And the damsel's father shall say unto the elders, I gave my daughter unto this man to wife, and he hateth her;

17   And, lo, he hath given occasions of speech against her, saying, I found not thy daughter a maid; and yet these are the tokens of my daughter's virginity. And they shall spread the cloth before the elders of the city.

18   And the elders of that city shall take that man and chastise him;

19   And they shall amerce him in an hundred shekels of silver, and give them unto the father of the damsel, because he hath

brought up an evil name upon a virgin of Israel: and she shall be his wife; he may not put her away all his days.

20 But if this thing be true, and the tokens of virginity be not found for the damsel:

21 Then they shall bring out the damsel to the door of her father's house, and the men of her city shall stone her with stones that she die: because she hath wrought folly in Israel, to play the whore in her father's house: so shalt thou put evil away from among you.

Deuteronomy 25
5 If brethren dwell together, and one of them die, and have no child, the wife of the dead shall not marry without unto a stranger: her husband's brother shall go in unto her, and take her to him to wife, and perform the duty of an husband's brother unto her.

6 And it shall be, that the firstborn which she beareth shall succeed in the name of his brother which is dead, that his name be not put out of Israel.

7 And if the man like not to take his brother's wife, then let his brother's wife go up to the gate unto the elders, and say, My husband's brother refuseth to raise up unto his brother a name in Israel, he will not perform the duty of my husband's brother.

8   Then the elders of his city shall call him, and speak unto him: and if he stand to it, and say, I like not to take her;

9   Then shall his brother's wife come unto him in the presence of the elders, and loose his shoe from off his foot, and spit in his face, and shall answer and say, So shall it be done unto that man that will not build up his brother's house.

10   And his name shall be called in Israel, The house of him that hath his shoe loosed.

Deuteronomy 25

11   When men strive together one with another, and the wife of the one draweth near for to deliver her husband out of the hand of him that smiteth him, and putteth forth her hand, and taketh him by the secrets:

12   Then thou shalt cut off her hand, thine eye shall not pity her.

Chapter 3-Son

Exodus 21

15 And he that smiteth his father, or his mother, shall be surely put to death.

Exodus 21

17 And he that curseth his father, or his mother, shall surely be put to death.

Exodus 22

29 Thou shalt not delay to offer the first of thy ripe fruits, and of thy liquors: the firstborn of thy sons shalt thou give unto me.

30 Likewise shalt thou do with thine oxen, and with thy sheep: seven days it shall be with his dam; on the eighth day thou shalt give it me.

Deuteronomy 21

18 If a man have a stubborn and rebellious son, which will not obey the voice of his father, or the voice of his mother, and that, when they have chastened him, will not hearken unto them:

19 Then shall his father and his mother lay hold on him, and bring him out unto the elders of his city, and unto the gate of his place;

20 And they shall say unto the elders of his city, This our son is stubborn and rebellious,

he will not obey our voice; he is a glutton, and a drunkard.

21 And all the men of his city shall stone him with stones, that he die: so shalt thou put evil away from among you; and all Israel shall hear, and fear.

Chapter 4-Daughter

Exodus 21

7   And if a man sell his daughter to be a maidservant, she shall not go out as the menservants do.

8   If she please not her master, who hath betrothed her to himself, then shall he let her be redeemed: to sell her unto a strange nation he shall have no power, seeing he hath dealt deceitfully with her.

9   And if he have betrothed her unto his son, he shall deal with her after the maimer of daughters.

10   If he take him another wife; her food, her raiment, and her duty of marriage, shall he not diminish.

11   And if he do not these three unto her, then shall she go out free without money.

Chapter 5-Adultery

Exodus 20
14   Thou shalt not commit adultery.

Leviticus 20
10   And the man that committeth adultery with another man's wife, even he that committeth adultery with his neighbour's wife, the adulterer and the adulteress shall surely be put to death.

Deuteronomy 18
18 Neither shalt thou commit adultery.

Deuteronomy 22
22 If a man be found lying with a woman married to an husband, then they shall both of them die, both the man that lay with the woman, and the woman: so shalt thou put away evil from Israel.

Deuteronomy 23
23 If a damsel that is a virgin be betrothed unto an husband, and a man find her in the city, and lie with her;

24 Then ye shall bring them both out unto the gate of that city, and ye shall stone them with stones that they die; the damsel, because she cried not being in the city; and the man, because he hath humbled his neighbour's wife: so thou shalt put away evil from among you.

Chapter 6-Elders

Leviticus 19

32 Thou shalt rise up before the hoary head, and honour the face of the old man, and fear thy God: I am the Lord.

Chapter 7-Divorce

Deuteronomy 24

1 When a man hath taken a wife, and married her, and it come to pass that she find no favour in his eyes, because he hath found some uncleanness in her: then let him write her a bill of divorcement, and give it in her hand, and send her out of his house.

2 And when she is departed out of his house, she may go and be another man's wife.

3 And if the latter husband hate her, and write her a bill of divorcement, and giveth it in her hand, and sendeth her out of his house; or if the latter husband die, which took her to be his wife;

4 Her former husband, which sent her away, may not take her again to be his wife, after that she is defiled; for that is abomination before the LORD: and thou shalt not cause the land to sin, which the LORD thy God giveth thee for an inheritance.

Chapter 8-A Jealous Husband

Numbers 5

11 And the LORD spake unto Moses, saying,

12 Speak unto the children of Israel, and say unto them, If any man's wife go aside, and commit an trespass against him,

13 And a man lie with her carnally, and it be hid from the eyes of her husband, and be kept close, and she be defiled, and there be no witness against her, neither she be taken with the manner;

14 And the spirit of jealousy come upon him, and he be jealous of his wife, and she be defiled: or if the spirit of jealousy come upon him, and he be jealous of his wife, and she be not defiled:

15 Then shall the man bring his wife unto the priest, and he shall bring her offering' for her, the tenth part of an ephah of barley meal; he shall pour no oil upon it, nor put frankincense thereon; for it is an offering of

jealousy, an offering of memorial, bringing iniquity to remembrance.

16 And the priest shall bring her near, and set her before the LORD:

17 And the priest shall take holy water in an earthen vessel; and of the dust that is in the floor of the tabernacle the priest shall take, and put it into the water:

18 And the priest shall set the woman before the LORD, and uncover the woman's head, and put the offering of memorial in her hands, which is the jealousy offering: and the priest shall have in his hand the bitter water that causeth the curse:

19 And the priest shall charge her by an oath, and say unto the woman, If no man have lain with thee, and if thou hast not gone aside to uncleanness with another instead of thy husband, be thou free from this bitter water that causeth the curse:

20 But if thou hast gone aside to another instead of thy husband, and if thou be defiled, and some man have lain with thee beside thine husband:

21 Then the priest shall charge the woman with an oath of cursing, and the priest shall say unto the woman, The LORD make thee a curse and an oath among thy people, when the LORD doth make thy thigh to rot, and thy belly to swell;

22 And this water that causeth the curse shall go into thy bowels, to make thy belly to swell, and thy thigh to rot: And the woman shall say,Amen, amen.

23 And the priest shall write these curses m a book, and he shall blot them out with the bitter water:

24 And he shall cause the woman to drink the bitter water that causeth the curse: and the water that causeth the curse shall enter into her, and become bitter.

25 Then the priest shall take the jealousy offering out of the woman's hand, and shall wave the offering before the LORD, and offer it upon the altar:

26 And the priest shall take an handful of the offering, even the memorial thereof, and burn it upon the altar, and afterward shall cause the woman to drink the water.

27 And when he hath made her to drink the water, then it shall come to pass, that, if she be defiled, and have done trespass against her husband, that the water that causeth the curse shall enter into her, and become bitter, and her belly shall swell, and her thigh shall rot: and the woman shall be a curse among her people.

28 And if the woman be not defiled, but be clean; then she shall be free, and shall conceive seed.

29 This is the law of jealousies, when a wife goeth aside to another instead of her husband, and is defiled;

30 Or when the spirit of jealousy cometh upon him, and he be jealous over his wife, and shall set the woman before the LORD, and the priest shall execute upon her all this law.

31 Then shall the man be guiltless from iniquity, and this woman shall bear her iniquity.

TITLE 4 – JUSTICE SYSTEM

Leviticus 24

22 Ye shall have one manner of law, as well for the stranger, as for one of your own country: for I am the LORD your God.

Chapter 1-Judges

Deuteronomy 16

18 Judges and officers shalt thou make thee in all thy gates, which the LORD thy God giveth thee, throughout thy tribes: and they shall judge the people with just judgment.

19 Thou shalt not wrest judgment; thou shalt not respect persons, neither take a gift: for a gift doth blind the eyes of the wise, and pervert the words of the righteous.

20 That which is altogether just shalt thou follow, that thou mayest live, and inherit the land which the LORD thy God giveth thee.

Deuteronomy 17

8   If there arise a matter too hard for thee in judgment, between blood and blood, between plea and plea, and between stroke and stroke, being matters of controversy within thy gates: then shalt thou arise, and get thee up into the place which the LORD thy God shall choose;

9   And thou shalt come unto the priests the Levites, and unto the judge that shall be

in those days, and inquire; and they shall shew thee the sentence of judgment:

10 And thou shalt do according to the sentence, which they of that place which the LORD shall choose shall shew thee; and thou shalt observe to do according to all that they inform thee:

11 According to the sentence of the law which they shall teach thee, and according to the judgment which they shall tell thee, thou shalt do: thou shalt not decline from the sentence which they shall shew thee, to the right hand, nor to the left.

12 And the man that will do presumptuously, and will not hearken unto the priest that standeth to minister there before the LORD thy God, or unto the judge, even that man shall die: and thou shalt put away the evil from Israel.

13 And all the people shall hear, and fear, and do no more presumptuously.

Chapter 2-Court

Exodus 23
2   Thou shalt not follow a multitude to do evil; neither shalt thou speak in a cause to decline after many to wrest judgment:

Exodus 23
3   Neither shalt thou countenance a poor man in his cause.

Exodus 23
6   Thou shalt not wrest the judgment of thy poor in his cause.

Exodus 23
7   Keep thee far from a false matter; and the innocent and righteous slay thou not: for I will not justify the wicked.

Exodus 23
8   And thou shalt take no gift: for the gift blindeth the wise, and perverteth the words of the righteous.

The Hebrew Israelite Law Book

Chapter 3-Witnesses

Exodus 20
16 Thou shalt not bear false witness against thy neighbour.

Exodus 23
1   Thou shalt not raise a false report: put not thine hand with the wicked to be an unrighteous witness.

Deuteronomy 5
20 Neither shalt thou bear false witness against thy neighbour.

Deuteronomy 19
15   One witness shall not rise up against a man for any iniquity, or for any sin, in any sin that he sinneth: at the mouth of two witnesses, or at the mouth of three witnesses, shall the matter be established.
16   If a false witness rise up against any man to testify against him that which is wrong;
17   Then both the men, between whom the controversy is, shall stand before the LORD,

before the priests and the judges, which shall be in those days;

18 And the judges shall make diligent inquisition: and, behold, if the witness be a false witness, and hath testified falsely against his brother;

19 Then shall ye do unto him, as he had thought to have done unto his brother: so shalt thou put the evil away from among you.

20 And those which remain shall hear, and fear, and shall henceforth commit no more any such evil among you.

21 And thine eye shall not pity; but life shall go for life, eye for eye, tooth for tooth, hand for hand, foot for foot.

Chapter 4-Judgments

Leviticus 19

15 Ye shall do no unrighteousness in judgment: thou shalt not respect the person of the poor, nor honour the person of the mighty: but in righteousness shalt thou judge thy neighbour.

Deuteronomy 24

17   Thou shalt not pervert the judgment of the stranger, nor of the fatherless; nor take a widow's raiment to pledge:

18   But thou shalt remember that thou wast a bondman in Egypt, and the LORD thy God redeemed thee thence: therefore I command thee to do this thing.

Chapter 5-Punishment

Numbers 5

5   And the LORD spake unto Moses, saying,

6   Speak unto the children of Israel, When a man or woman shall commit any sin that men commit, to do a trespass against the LORD, and that person be guilty;

7   Then they shall confess their sin which they have done: and he shall recompense his trespass with the principal thereof, and add unto it the fifth part thereof, and give it unto him against whom he hath trespassed.

8   But if the man have no kinsman to recompense the trespass unto, let the trespass be recompensed unto the LORD, even to the priest; beside the ram of the atonement, whereby an atonement shall be made for him.

9   And every offering of all the holy things of the children of Israel, which they bring unto the priest, shall be his.

10   And every man's hallowed things shall be his: whatsoever any man giveth the priest, it shall be his.

Deuteronomy 21

22 And if a man have committed a sin worthy of death, and he be to be put to death, and thou hang him on a tree:

23 His body shall not remain all night upon the tree, but thou shalt in any wise bury him that day; (for he that is hanged is accursed of God;) that thy land be not defiled, which the LORD thy God giveth thee for an inheritance.

Deuteronomy 24

16 The fathers shall not be put to death for the children, neither shall the children be put to death for the fathers: every man shall be put to death for his own sin.

Deuteronomy 25

1 If there be a controversy between men, and they come unto judgment, that the judges may judge them; then they shall justify the righteous, and
condemn the wicked.

2 And it shall be, if the wicked man be worthy to be beaten, that the judge shall cause him to lie down, and to be beaten before his face, according to his fault, by a certain number.

3 Forty stripes he may give him, and not exceed: lest, if he should exceed, and beat him

above these with many stripes, then thy brother should seem vile unto thee.

Chapter 6-Cities of Refuge for Murder

Numbers 35

9 And the LORD spake unto Moses, saying,

10 Speak unto the children of Israel, and say unto them, When ye be come over Jordan into the land of Canaan;

11 Then ye shall appoint you cities to be cities of refuge for you; that the slayer may flee thither, which killeth any person at unawares.

12 And they shall be unto you cities for refuge from the avenger; that the manslayer die not, until he stand before the congregation in judgment.

13 And of these cities which ye shall give six cities shall ye have for refuge.

14 Ye shall give three cities on this side Jordan, and three cities shall ye give in the land of Canaan, which shall be cities of refuge.

15 These six cities shall be a refuge, both for the children of Israel, and for the stranger,

and for the sojourner among them: that every one that killeth any person unawares may flee thither.

16 And if he smite him with an instrument of iron, so that he die, he is a murderer: the murderer shall surely be put to death.

17 And if he smite him with throwing a stone, wherewith he may die, and he die, he is a murderer: the murderer shall surely be put to death.

18 Or if he smite him with an hand weapon of wood, wherewith he may die, and he die, he is a murderer: the murderer shall surely be put to death.

19 The revenger of blood himself shall slay the murderer: when he meeteth him, he shall slay him.

20 But if he thrust him of hatred, or hurl at him by laying of wait, that he die;

21 Or in enmity smite him with his hand, that he die: he that smote him shall surely be put to death; for he is a murderer: the revenger of blood shall slay the murderer, when he meeteth him.

22 But if he thrust him suddenly without enmity, or have cast upon him any thing without laying of wait,

23 Or with any stone, where-with a man may die, seeing him not, and cast it upon him,

that he die, and was not his enemy, neither sought his harm:

24 Then the congregation shall judge between the slayer and the revenger of blood according to these judgments:

25 And the congregation shall deliver the slayer out of the hand of the revenger of blood, and the congregation shall restore him to the city of his refuge, whither he was fled: and he shall abide in it unto the death of the high priest, which was anointed with the holy oil.

26 But if the slayer shall at any time come without the border of the city of his refuge, whither he was fled;

27 And the revenger of blood find him without the borders of the city of his refuge, and the revenger of blood kill the slayer; he shall not be guilty of blood:

28 Because he should have remained in the city of his refuge until the death of the high priest: but after the death of the high priest the slayer shall return into the land of his possession.

29 So these things shall be for a statute of judgment unto you throughout your generations in all your dwellings.

Chapter 7-King

Deuteronomy 17

14 When thou art come unto the land which the LORD thy God giveth thee, and shalt possess it, and shalt dwell therein, and shalt say, I will set a king over me, like as all the nations that are about me;

15 Thou shalt in any wise set him king over thee, whom the LORD thy God shall choose: one from among thy brethren shalt thou set king over thee: thou mayest not set a stranger over thee, which is not thy brother.

16 But he shall not multiply horses to himself, nor cause the people to return to Egypt, to the end that he should multiply horses: forasmuch as the LORD hath said unto you, Ye shall henceforth return no more that way.

17 Neither shall he multiply wives to himself, that his heart turn not away: neither shall he greatly multiply to himself silver and gold.

18 And it shall be, when he sitteth upon the throne of his kingdom, that he shall write

him a copy of this law in a book out of that which is before the priests the Levites:

19 And it shall be with him, and he shall read therein all the days of his life: that he may learn to fear the LORD his God, to keep all the words of this law and these statutes, to do them:

20 That his heart be not lifted up above his brethren, and that he turn not aside from the commandment, to the right hand, or to the left: to the end that he may prolong his days in his kingdom, he, and his children, in the midst of Israel.

The Hebrew Israelite Law Book

TITLE 5 – NAKEDNESS

Leviticus 18

6   None of you shall approach to any that is near of kin to him, to uncover their nakedness: I am the Lord.

7   The nakedness of thy father, or the nakedness of thy mother, shalt thou not uncover: she is thy mother; thou shalt not uncover her nakedness.

8   The nakedness of thy father's wife shalt thou not uncover: it is thy father's nakedness.

9   The nakedness of thy sister, the daughter of thy father, or daughter of thy mother, whether she be bom at home, or bom abroad, even their nakedness thou shalt not uncover.

10   The nakedness of thy son's daughter, or of thy daughter's daughter, even their nakedness thou shalt not uncover: for theirs is thine own nakedness.

11   The nakedness of thy father's wife's daughter, begotten of thy father, she is thy sister, thou shalt not uncover her nakedness.

12　Thou shalt not uncover the nakedness of thy father's sister: she is thy father's near kinswoman.

13　Thou shalt not uncover the nakedness of thy mother's sister: for she is thy mother's near kinswoman.

14　Thou shalt not uncover the nakedness of thy father's brother, thou shalt not approach to his wife: she is thine aunt.

15　Thou shalt not uncover the nakedness of thy daughter in law: she is thy son's wife; thou shalt not uncover her nakedness.

16　Thou shalt not uncover the nakedness of thy brother's wife: it is thy brother's nakedness.

17　Thou shalt not uncover the nakedness of a woman and her daughter, neither shalt thou take her son's daughter, or her daughter's daughter, to uncover her nakedness; for they are her near kinswomen: it is wickedness.

18　Neither shalt thou take a wife to her sister, to vex her, to uncover her nakedness, beside the other in her life time.

19 Also thou shalt not approach unto a woman to uncover her nakedness, as long as she is put apart for her uncleanness.

The Hebrew Israelite Law Book

TITLE 6 – WHORISH ACTIONS

Chapter 1-Lying With

Exodus 22

16 And if a man entice a maid that is not betrothed, and lie with her, he shall surely endow her to be his wife.

17 If her father utterly refuse to give her unto him, he shall pay money according to the dowry of virgins.

Leviticus 19

20 And whosoever lieth carnally with a woman, that is a bondmaid, betrothed to an husband, and not at all redeemed, nor freedom given her; she shall be scourged; they shall not be put to death, because she was not free.

21 And he shall bring his trespass offering unto the LORD, unto the door of the tabernacle of the congregation, even a ram for a trespass offering.

22 And the priest shall make an atonement for him with the ram of the trespass offering before the LORD for his sin which he hath done: and the sin which he hath done shall be forgiven him.

Leviticus 20

11   And the man that lieth with his father's wife hath uncover

ed his father's nakedness: both of them shall surely be put to death; their blood shall be upon them.

12 And if a man lie with his daughter in law, both of them shall surely be put to death: they have wrought confusion; their blood shall be upon them.

Leviticus 20

14 And if a man take a wife and her mother, it is wickedness: they shall be burnt with fire, both he and they; that there be no wickedness among you.

Leviticus 20

18 And if a man shall lie with a woman having her sickness, and shall uncover her nakedness; he hath discovered her fountain, and she hath uncovered the fountain of her blood: and both of them shall be cut off from among their people.

Leviticus 20

20 And if a man shall lie with his uncle's wife, he hath uncovered his uncle's nakedness: they shall bear their sin; they shall die childless.

Deuteronomy 23

28 If a man find a damsel that is a virgin, which is not betrothed, and lay hold on her, and lie with her, and they be found;

29 Then the man that lay with her shall give unto the damsel's father fifty shekels of silver, and she shall be his wife; because he hath humbled her, he may not put her away all his days.

Chapter 2-Homosexuality

Leviticus 18
22 Thou shalt not lie with mankind, as with womankind: it is abomination.

Leviticus 20
13 If a man also lie with mankind, as he lieth with a woman, both of them have committed an abomination: they shall surely be put to death; their blood shall be upon them.

The Hebrew Israelite Law Book

Chapter 3-Fornication

Leviticus 18
20 Moreover thou shalt not lie carnally with thy neighbour's wife, to defile thyself with her.

Deuteronomy 22
30 A man shall not take his father's wife, nor discover his father's skirt.

Chapter 4-Bestiality

Exodus 22

19 Whosoever lieth with a beast shall surely be put to death.

Leviticus 18

23 Neither shalt thou lie with any beast to defile thyself therewith: neither shall any woman stand before a beast to lie down thereto: it is confusion.

24 Defile not ye yourselves in any of these things: for in all these the nations are defiled which I cast out before you:

25 And the land is defiled: therefore I do visit the iniquity thereof upon it, and the land itself vomiteth out her inhabitants.

26 Ye shall therefore keep my statutes and my judgments, and shall not commit any of these abominations; neither any of your own nation, nor any stranger that sojourneth among you:

27 (For all these abominations have the men of the land done, which were before you, and the land is defiled;)

28 That the land spue not you out also, when ye defile it, as it spued out the nations that were before you.

29 For whosoever shall commit any of these abominations, even the souls that commit them shall be cut off from among their people.

30 Therefore shall ye keep mine ordinance, that ye commit not any one of these abominable customs, which were committed before you, and that ye defile not yourselves therein: I am the Lord your God.

Leviticus 20

15 And if a man lie with a beast, he shall surely be put to death: and ye shall slay the beast.

16 And if a woman approach unto any beast, and lie down thereto, thou shalt kill the woman, and the beast: they shall surely be put to death; their blood shall be upon them.

Chapter 5-Whoring

Leviticus 19

29 Do not prostitute thy daughter, to cause her to be a whore; lest the land fall to whoredom, and the land become full of wickedness.

Deuteronomy 23

11 There shall be no whore of the daughters of Israel, nor a sodomite of the sons of Israel.

Deuteronomy 23

12 Thou shalt not bring the hire of a whore, or the price of a dog, into the house of the LORD thy God for any vow: for even both these are abomination unto the LORD thy God.

Chapter 6-Nakedness

Leviticus 20

17   And if a man shall take his sister, his father's daughter, or his mother's daughter, and see her nakedness, and she see his nakedness; it is a wicked thing; and they shall be cut off in the sight of their people: he hath uncovered his sister's nakedness; he shall bear his iniquity.

Leviticus 20

19 And thou shalt not uncover the nakedness of thy mother's sister, nor of thy father's sister: for he uncovereth his near kin: they shall bear their iniquity.

Leviticus 20

21   And if a man shall take his brother's wife, it is an unclean thing: he hath uncovered his brother's nakedness; they shall be childless.

The Hebrew Israelite Law Book

The Hebrew Israelite Law Book

The Hebrew Israelite Law Book

TITLE 7 – CRUELTY

Chapter 1-Mental Cruelty

Exodus 20

17 Thou shalt not covet thy neighbour's house, thou shalt not covet thy neighbour's wife, nor his manservant, nor his maidservant, nor his ox, nor his ass, nor any thing that is thy neighbour's.

Exodus 22

22 Ye shall not afflict any widow, or fatherless child.

23 If thou afflict them in any wise, and they cry at all unto me, I will surely hear their cry;

24 And my wrath shall wax hot, and I will kill you with the sword; and your wives shall be widows, and your children fatherless.

Exodus 22

22 Ye shall not afflict any widow, or fatherless child.

Exodus 22

28 Thou shalt not revile the gods, nor curse the ruler of thy people.

Exodus 23
4   If thou meet thine enemy's ox or his ass going astray, thou shalt surely bring it back to him again.

Exodus 23
5   If thou see the ass of him that hateth thee lying under his burden, and wouldest forbear to help him, thou shalt surely help with him.

Leviticus 19
14   Thou shalt not curse the deaf, nor put a stumblingblock before the blind, but shalt fear thy God: I am the LORD.

Leviticus 19
18   Thou shalt not avenge, nor bear any grudge against the children of thy people, but thou shalt love thy neighbour as thyself: I am the LORD.

Chapter 2-Verbal Cruelty

Leviticus 19

16 Thou shalt not go up and down as a talebearer among thy people: neither shalt thou stand against the blood of thy neighbour: I am the LORD.

17 Thou shalt not hate thy brother in thine heart: thou shalt in any wise rebuke thy neighbour, and not suffer sin upon him.

TITLE 8 – COVETOUSNESS

Exodus 20

17 Thou shalt not covet thy neighbour's house, thou shalt not covet thy neighbour's wife, nor his manservant, nor his maidservant, nor his ox, nor his ass, nor any thing that is thy neighbour's.

Deuteronomy 5

21 Neither shalt thou desire thy neighbour's wife, neither shalt thou covet thy neighbour's house, his field, or his manservant, or his maidservant, his ox, or his ass, or any thing that is thy neighbour's.

The Hebrew Israelite Law Book

The Hebrew Israelite Law Book

TITLE 9 - ASSAULT

Exodus 21

15   And he that smiteth his father, or his mother, shall be surely put to death.

Exodus 21

18   And if men strive together, and one smite another with a stone, or with his fist, and he die not, but keepeth his bed:

19   If he rise again, and walk abroad upon his staff, then shall he that smote him be quit: only he shall pay for the loss of his time, and shall cause him to be thoroughly healed.

Exodus 21

20   And if a man smite his servant, or his maid, with a rod, and he die under his hand; he shall be surely punished.

21   Notwithstanding, if he continue a day or two, he shall not be punished: for he is his money.

Exodus 21

22   If men strive, and hurt a woman with child, so that her fruit depart from her, and

yet no mischief follow: he shall be surely punished, according as the woman's husband will lay upon him; and he shall pay as the judges determine.

23 And if any mischief follow, then thou shalt give life for life,

24 Eye for eye, tooth for tooth, hand for hand, foot for foot,

25 Burning for burning, wound for wound, stripe for stripe.

Exodus 21

26 And if a man smite the eye of his servant, or the eye of his maid, that it perish; he shall let him go free for his eye's sake.

27 And if he smite out his manservant's tooth, or his maidservant's tooth; he shall let him go free for his tooth's sake.

Exodus 21

28 If an ox gore a man or a woman, that they die: then the ox shall be surely stoned, and his flesh shall not be eaten; but the owner of the ox shall be quit.

29 But if the ox were wont to push with his horn in time past, and it hath been testified to his owner, and he hath not kept him in, but that he hath killed a man or a woman; the ox shall be stoned, and his owner also shall be put to death.

30 If there be laid on him a sum of money, then he shall give for the ransom of his life whatsoever is laid upon him.

31 Whether he have gored a son, or have gored a daughter, according to this judgment shall it be done unto him.

Exodus 21

32 If the ox shall push a manservant or a maidservant; he shall give unto their master thirty shekels of silver, and the ox shall be stoned.

Leviticus 24

19 And if a man cause a blemish in his neighbour; as he hath done, so shall it be done to him;

20 Breach for breach, eye for eye, tooth for tooth: as he hath caused a blemish in a man, so shall it be done to him again.

Deuteronomy 23

25 But if a man find a betrothed damsel in the field, and the man force her, and lie with her: then the man only that lay with her shall die:

26 But unto the damsel thou shalt do nothing; there is in the damsel no sin worthy of death: for as when a man riseth against his

neighbour, and slayeth him, even so is this matter:

27 For he found her in the field, and the betrothed damsel cried, and there was none to save her.

Deuteronomy 24

7 If a man be found stealing any of his brethren of the children of Israel, and maketh merchandise of him, or selleth him; then that thief shall die; and thou shalt put evil away from among you.

The Hebrew Israelite Law Book

TITLE 10 - THEFT

Exodus 20
15   Thou shalt not steal.

Exodus 21
16   And he that stealeth a man, and selleth him, or if he be found in his hand, he shall surely be put to death.

Exodus 22
1   If a man shall steal an ox, or a sheep, and kill it, or sell it; he shall restore five oxen for an ox, and four sheep for a sheep.

Exodus 22
2   If a thief be found breaking up, and be smitten that he die, there shall no blood be shed for him.
3   If the sun be risen upon him, there shall be blood shed for him; for he should make full restitution; if he have nothing, then he shall be sold for his theft.
4   If the theft be certainly found in his hand alive, whether it be ox, or ass, or sheep; he shall restore double.

Exodus 22

5   If a man shall cause a field or vineyard to be eaten, and shall put in his beast, and shall feed in another man's field; of the best of his own field, and of the best of his own vineyard, shall he make restitution.

Exodus 22

7   If a man shall deliver unto his neighbour money or stuff to keep, and it be stolen out of the man's house; if the thief be found, let him pay double.
8   If the thief be not found, then the master of the house shall be brought unto the judges, to see whether he have put his hand unto his neighbour's goods.

Exodus 22

9   For all manner of trespass, whether it be for ox, for ass, for sheep, for raiment, or for any manner of lost thing, which another challengeth to be his, the cause of both parties shall come before the judges; and whom the judges shall condemn, he shall pay double unto his neighbour.

Leviticus 19

11 Ye shall not steal, neither deal falsely, neither lie one to another.

Leviticus 19

13 Thou shalt not defraud thy neighbour, neither rob him: the wages of him that is hired shall not abide with thee all night until the morning.

Deuteronomy 5

19 Neither shalt thou steal.

TITLE 11 - LIABILITY

Exodus 22

6   If fire break out, and catch in thorns, so that the stacks of corn, or the standing corn, or the field, be consumed there with; he that kindled the fire shall surely make restitution.

Exodus 22

10   If a man deliver unto his neighbour an ass, or an ox, or a sheep, or any beast, to keep;

and it die, or be hurt, or driven away, no man seeing it:

11　Then shall an oath of the Lord be between them both, that he hath not put his hand unto his neighbour's goods; and the owner of it shall accept thereof, and he shall not make it good.

12　And if it be stolen from him, he shall make restitution unto the owner thereof.

13　If it be torn in pieces, then let him bring it for witness, and he shall not make good that which was torn.

Exodus 22

14　And if a man borrow ought of his neighbour, and it be hurt, or die, the owner thereof being not with it, he shall surely make it good.

15　But if the owner thereof be with it, he shall not make it good: if it be an hired thing, it came for his hire.

Deuteronomy 22

8　When thou buildest a new house, then thou shalt make a battlement for thy roof, that thou bring not blood upon thine house, if any man fall from thence.

The Hebrew Israelite Law Book

The Hebrew Israelite Law Book

TITLE 12 - MURDER

Exodus 20
13 Thou shalt not kill

Exodus 21
12   He that smiteth a man, so that he die, shall be surely put to death.
13 And if a man lie not in wait, but God deliver him into his hand; then I will appoint thee a place whither he shall flee.
14 But if a man come presumptuously upon his neighbour, to slay him with guile; thou shalt take him from mine altar, that he may die.

Leviticus 24
17 And he that killeth any man shall surely be put to death.
18 And he that killeth a beast shall make it good; beast for beast

Leviticus 24
21 And he that killeth a beast he shall restore it: and he that killeth a man, he shall be put to death.

Numbers 36

30 Whoso killeth any person, the murderer shall be put to death by the mouth of witnesses: but one witness shall not testify against any person to cause him to die.

31 Moreover ye shall take no satisfaction for the life of a murderer, which is guilty of death: but he shall be surely put to death.

32 And ye shall take no satisfaction for him that is fled to the city of his refuge, that he should come again to dwell in the land, until the death of the priest.

33 So ye shall not pollute the land wherein ye are: for blood it defileth the land: and the land cannot be cleansed of the blood that is shed therein, but by the blood of him that shed it.

34 Defile not therefore the land which ye shall inhabit, wherein I dwell: for I the LORD dwell among the children of Israel.

Deuteronomy 5

17 Thou shalt not kill.

Deuteronomy 21

1 If one be found slain in the land which the LORD thy God giveth thee to possess it, lying in the field, and it be not known who hath slain him:

2   Then thy elders and thy judges shall come forth, and they shall measure unto the cities which are round about him that is slain:

3   And it shall be, that the city which is next unto the slain man, even the elders of that city shall take an heifer, which hath not been wrought with, and which hath not drawn in the yoke;

4   And the elders of that city shall bring down the heifer unto a rough valley, which is neither eared nor sown, and shall strike off the heifer's neck there in the valley:

5   And the priests the sons of Levi shall come near; for them the LORD thy God hath Chosen to minister unto him, and to bless in the name of the LORD ; and by their word shall every controversy and every stroke be tried:

6   And all the elders of that city, that are next unto the slain man, shall wash their hands over the heifer that is beheaded in the valley:

7   And they shall answer and say, Our hands have not shed this blood, neither have our eyes seen it.

8   Be merciful, O LORD, unto thy people Israel, whom thou hast redeemed, and lay not innocent blood unto thy people of Israel's charge. And the blood shall be forgiven them.

9 So shalt thou put away the guilt of innocent blood from among you, when thou shalt do that which is right in the sight of the LORD.

TITLE 13 – APPEARANCE

Leviticus 19

27 Ye shall not round the corners of your heads, neither shalt thou mar the corners of thy beard.

28 Ye shall not make any cuttings in your flesh for the dead, nor print any marks upon you: I am the LORD.

Numbers 15

37 And the LORD spake unto Moses, saying,

38 Speak unto the children of Israel, and bid them that they make them fringes in the borders of their garments throughout their generations, and that they put upon the fringe of the borders a ribband of blue:

39 And it shall be unto you for a fringe, that ye may look upon it, and remember all the commandments of the LORD, and do them; and that ye seek not after your own heart and your own eyes, after which ye use to go a whoring:

40 That ye may remember, and do all my commandments, and be holy unto your God.

41 I am the LORD your God, which brought you out of the land of Egypt, to be your God: I am the LORD your God.

Deuteronomy 14

1 Ye are the children of the Lord your God: ye shall not cut yourselves, nor make any baldness between your eyes for the dead.

2 For thou art an holy people unto the LORD thy God, and the LORD hath chosen thee to be a peculiar people unto himself, above all the nations that are upon the earth.

Deuteronomy 22

5 The woman shall not wear that which pertaineth unto a man, neither shall a man put on a woman's garment: for all that do so are abomination unto the LORD thy God.

Deuteronomy 22

11 Thou shalt not wear a garment of divers sorts, as of woollen and linen together.

Deuteronomy 22

12 Thou shalt make thee fringes upon the four quarters of thy vesture, wherewith thou coverest thyself.

The Hebrew Israelite Law Book

TITLE 14 - STRANGERS

Exodus 22

21 Thou shalt neither vex a stranger, nor oppress him: for ye were strangers in the land of Egypt.

Exodus 23

9 Also thou shalt not oppress a stranger: for ye know the heart of a stranger, seeing ye were strangers in the land of Egypt.

Leviticus 19

33 And if a stranger sojourn with thee in your land, ye shall not vex him.

34   But the stranger that dwelleth with you shall be unto you as one born among you, and thou shalt love him as thyself; for ye were strangers in the land of Egypt: I am the LORD your God.

The Hebrew Israelite Law Book

TITLE 15 – HELPING A BROTHER

Deuteronomy 22

1   Thou shalt not see thy brother's ox or his sheep go astray, and hide thyself from them: thou shalt in any case bring them again unto thy brother.

2 And if thy brother be not nigh unto thee, or if thou know him not, then thou shalt bring it unto thine own house, and it shall be with thee until thy brother seek after it, and thou shalt restore it to him again.

3   In like manner shalt thou do with his ass; and so shalt thou do with his raiment; and with all lost thing of thy brother's, which he hath lost, and thou hast found, shalt thou do likewise : thou mayest not hide thyself.

4   Thou shalt not see thy brother's ass or his ox fall down by the way, and hide thyself from them; thou shalt surely help him to lift them up again.

The Hebrew Israelite Law Book

TITLE 16 – TABERNACLE

Exodus 40

1   And the LORD spake unto Moses, saying,

2   On the first day of the first month shalt thou set up the tabernacle of the tent of the congregation.

3   And thou shalt put therein the ark of the testimony, and cover the ark with the vail.

4   And thou shalt bring in the table, and set in order the things that are to be set in order upon it; and thou shalt bring in the candlestick, and light the lamps thereof.

5   And thou shalt set the altar of gold for the incense before the ark of the testimony, and put the hanging of the door to the tabernacle.

6   And thou shalt set the altar of the burnt offering before the door of the tabernacle of the tent of the congregation.

7   And thou shalt set the laver between the tent of the congregation and the altar, and shalt put water therein.

8   And thou shalt set up the court round about, and hang up the hanging at the court gate.

9   And thou shalt take the anointing oil, and anoint the tabernacle, and all that is therein, and shalt hallow it, and all the vessels thereof: and it shall be holy.

10   And thou shalt anoint the altar of the burnt offering, and all his vessels, and sanctify the altar: and it shall be an altar most holy.

11   And thou shalt anoint the laver and his foot, and sanctify it.

12   And thou shalt bring Aaron and his sons unto the door of the tabernacle of the congregation, and wash them with water.

13   And thou shalt put upon Aaron the holy garments, and anoint him, and sanctify him; that he may minister unto me in the priest's office.

14   And thou shalt bring his sons, and clothe them with coats:

15   And thou shalt anoint them, as thou didst anoint their father, that they may minister unto me in the priest's office: for their anointing shall surely be an everlasting priesthood throughout their generations.

16 Thus did Moses: according to all that the LORD commanded him, so did he.

17 And it came to pass in the first month in the second year, on the first day of the month, that the tabernacle was reared up.

18 And Moses reared up the tabernacle, and fastened his sockets, and set up the boards thereof, and put in the bars thereof, and reared up his pillars.

19 And he spread abroad the tent over the tabernacle, and put the covering of the tent above upon it; as the LORD commanded Moses.

20 And he took and put the testimony into the ark, and set the staves on the ark, and put the mercy seat above upon the ark:

21 And he brought the ark into the tabernacle, and set up the vail of the covering, and covered the ark of the testimony; as the LORD commanded Moses.

22 And he put the table in the tent of the congregation, upon the side of the tabernacle northward, without the vail.

23 And he set the bread in order upon it before the LORD; as the LORD had commanded Moses.

24 And he put the candlestick in the tent of the congregation, over against the table, on the side of the tabernacle southward.

25 And he lighted the lamps before the LORD; as the LORD commanded Moses.

26 And he put the golden altar in the tent of the congregation before the vail:

27 And he burnt sweet incense thereon; as the LORD commanded Moses.

28 And he set up the hanging at the door of the tabernacle.

29 And he put the altar of burnt offering by the door of the tabernacle of the tent of the congregation, and offered upon it the burnt offering and the meat offering; as the LORD commanded Moses.

30 And he set the laver between the tent of the congregation and the altar, and put water there, to wash withal.

31 And Moses and Aaron and his sons washed their hands and their feet threat:

32 When they went into the tent of the congregation, and when they came near unto the altar, they washed; as the LORD commanded Moses.

33 And he reared up the court round about the tabernacle and the altar, and set up the hanging of the court gate. So Moses finished the work.

Chapter 1 – Offerings for the Tabernacle and Priesthood

Exodus 25

1 And the LORD spake unto Moses, saying,

2 Speak unto the children of Israel, that they bring me an offering: of every man that giveth it willingly with his heart ye shall take my offering.

3 And this is the offering which ye shall take of them; gold, and silver, and brass,

4 And blue, and purple, and scarlet, and fine linen, and goats' hair,

5 And rams' skins dyed red, and badgers' skins, and shittim wood,

6 Oil for the light, spices for anointing oil, and for sweet in-cense,

7 Onyx stones, and stones to be set in the ephod, and in the breastplate.

8 And let them make me a sanctuary; that I may dwell among them.

9   According to all that I shew thee, after the pattern of the tabernacle, and the pattern of all the instruments thereof, even so shall ye make it.

Exodus 26
30 And thou shalt rear up the tabernacle according to the fashion thereof which was shewed thee in the mount.

Exodus 27
19 All the vessels of the tabernacle in all the service thereof, and all the pins thereof, and all the pins of the court, shall be of brass.

Exodus 31
1   And the LORD spake unto Moses, saying,
2   See, I have called by name Bezaleel the son of Uri, the son of Hur, of the tribe of Judah:
3   And I have filled him with the spirit of God, in wisdom, and in understanding, and in knowledge, and in all manner of workmanship,
4   To devise cunning works, to work in gold, and in silver, and in brass,
5   And in cutting of stones, to set them, and in carving of timber, to work in all manner of workmanship.

6   And I, behold, I have given with him Aholiab, the son of Ahisamach, of the tribe of Dan: and in the hearts of all that are wise hearted I have put wisdom, that they may make all that I have commanded thee;

7   The tabernacle of the congregation, and the ark of the testimony, and the mercy seat that is thereupon, and all the furniture of the tabernacle,

8   And the table and his furniture, and the pure candlestick with all his furniture, and the altar of incense,

9   And the altar of burnt offering with all his furniture, and the laver and his foot,

10 And the cloths of service, and the holy garments for Aaron the priest, and the garments of his sons, to minister in the priest's office,

11 And the anointing oil, and sweet incense for the holy place: according to all that I have commanded thee shall they do.

Exodus 35

4   And Moses spake unto all the congregation of the Children of Israel, saying, This is the thing which the LORD commanded, saying,

5   Take ye from among you an offering unto the LORD: whosoever is of a willing

heart, let him bring it, an offering of the LORD; gold, and silver, and brass,

6   And blue, and purple, and scarlet, and fine linen, and goats' hair,

7   And rams' skins dyed red, and badgers' skins, and shittim wood,

8   And oil for the light, and spices for anointing oil, and for the sweet incense,

9   And onyx stones, and stones to be set for the ephod, and for the breastplate.

10   And every wise hearted among you shall come, and make all that the LORD hath commanded;

11   The tabernacle, his tent, and his covering, his taches, and his boards, his bars, his pillars, and his sockets,

12   The ark, and the staves thereof, with the mercy seat, and the vail of the covering,

13   The table, and his staves, and all his vessels, and the shewbread,

14   The candlestick also for the light, and his furniture, and his lamps, with the oil for the light,

15   And the incense altar, and his staves, and the anointing oil, and the sweet incense, and the hanging for the door at the entering in of the tabernacle,

16   The altar of burnt offering, with his brasen grate, his staves, and all his vessels, the laver and his foot,

17 The hangings of the court, his pillars, and their sockets, and the hanging for the door of the court,

18 The pins of the tabernacle, and the pins of the court, and their cords,

19 The cloths of service, to do service in the holy place, the holy garments for Aaron the priest, and the garments of his sons, to minister in the priest's office.

20 And all the congregation of the children of Israel departed from the presence of Moses.

21 And they came, every one whose heart stirred him up, and every one whom his spirit made willing, and they brought the LORD'S offering to the work of the tabernacle of the congregation, and for all his service, and for the holy garments.

22 And they came, both men and women, as many as were willing hearted, and brought bracelets, and earrings, and rings, and tablets, all jewels of gold: and every man that offered offered an offering of gold unto the LORD.

23 And every man, with whom was found blue, and purple, and scarlet, and fine linen, and goats' hair, and red skins of rams, and badgers' skins, brought them.

24 Every one that did offer an offering of silver and brass brought the Lord's offering:

and every man, with whom was found shittim wood for any work of the service, brought it.

25 And all the women that were wise hearted did spin with their hands, and brought that which they had spun, both of blue, and of purple, and of scarlet, and of fine linen.

26 And all the women whose heart stirred them up in wisdom spun goats' hair.

27 And the rulers brought onyx stones, and stones to be set, for the ephod, and for the breastplate;

28 And spice, and oil for the light, and for the anointing oil, and for the sweet incense.

29 The children of Israel brought a willing offering unto the LORD, every man and woman, whose heart made them willing to bring for all manner of work, which the LORD had commanded to be made by the hand of Moses.

30 And Moses said unto the children of Israel, See, the LORD hath called by name Bezaleel the son of Uri, the son of Hur, of the tribe of Judah;

31 And he hath filled him with the spirit of God, in wisdom, in understanding, and in knowledge, and in all manner of workmanship;

32 And to devise curious works, to work in gold, and in silver, and in brass,

33 And in the cutting of stones, to set them, and in carving of wood, to make any manner of cunning work.

34 And he hath put in his heart that he may teach, both he, and Aholiab, the son of Ahisamch, of the tribe of Dan.

35 Them hath he filled with wisdom of heart, to work all manner of work, of the engraver, and of the cunning workman, and of the embroiderer, in blue, and in purple, in scarlet, and in fine linen, and of the weaver, even of them that do any work, and of those that devise cunning work.

Exodus 36

1 Then wrought Bezaleel and Aholiab, and every wise hearted man, in whom the LORD put wisdom and understanding to know how to work all manner of work for the service of the sanctuary, according to all that the LORD had commanded.

2 And Moses called Bezaleel and Aholiab, and every wise hearted man, in whose heart the LORD had put wisdom, even every one whose heart stirred him up to come unto the work to do it:

3 And they received of Moses all the offering, which the children of Israel had brought for the work of the service of the sanctuary, to make it withal. And they

brought yet unto him free offerings every morning.

4   And all the wise men, that wrought all the work of the sanctuary, came every man from his work which they made;

5   And they spake unto Moses, saying, The people bring much more than enough for the service of the work, which the LORD commanded to make.

6   And Moses gave commandment, and they caused it to be proclaimed throughout the camp, saying, Let neither man nor woman make any more work for the offering of the sanctuary. So the people were restrained from bringing.

7   For the stuff they had was sufficient for all the work to make it, and too much.

Exodus 38

21   This is the sum of the tabernacle, even of the tabernacle of testimony, as it was counted, according to the commandment of Moses, for the service of the Levites, by the hand of Ithamar, son to Aaron the priest.

22   And Bezaleel the son of Uri, the son of Hur, of the tribe of Judah, made all that the Lord commanded Moses.

23   And with him was Aholiab, son of Ahisamach, of the tribe of Dan, an engraver, and a cunning workman, and an embroiderer

in blue, and in purple, and in scarlet, and fine linen.

24 All the gold that was occupied for the work in all the work of the holy place, even the gold of the offering, was twenty and nine talents, and seven hundred and thirty shekels, after the she'-k61 of the sanctuary.

25 And the silver of them that were numbered of the congregation was an hundred talents, and a thousand seven hundred and threescore and fifteen shekels, after the shekels of the sanctuary:

26 A bekah for every man, that is, half a shekel, after the shekel of the sanctuary, for every one that went to be numbered, from twenty years old and upward, for six hundred thousand and three thousand and five hundred and fifty men,

27 And of the hundred talents of silver were cast the sockets of the sanctuary, and the sockets of the vail; an hundred sockets of the hundred talents, a talent for a socket.

28 And of the thousand seven hundred seventy and five shekels he made hooks for the pillars, and overlaid their chapiters, and filleted them.

29 And the brass of the offering was seventy talents, and two thousand and four hundred shekels.

30 And therewith he made the sockets to the door of the tabernacle of the congregation, and the brasen altar, and the brasen grate for it, and all the vessels of the altar,

31 And the sockets of the court round about, and the sockets of the court gate, and all the pins of the tabernacle, and all the pins of the court round about.

Chapter 39

1 And of the blue, and purple, and scarlet, they made cloths of service, to do service in the holy place, and made the holy garments for Aaron; as the Lord commanded Moses.

Chapter 2 - Tabernacle Curtains

A. Linen Tabernacle

Exodus 26

1 Moreover thou shalt make the tabernacle with ten curtains of fine twined linen, and blue, and purple, and scarlet: with cherubims of cunning work shalt thou make them.

2 The length of one curtain shall be eight and twenty cubits, and the breadth of one curtain four cubits: and every one of the curtains shall have one measure.

3 The five curtains shall be coupled together one to another; and other five curtains shall be coupled one to another.

4 And thou shalt make loops of blue upon the edge of the one curtain from the selvedge in the coupling; and likewise shalt thou make in the uttermost edge of another curtain, in the coupling of the second.

5 Fifty loops shalt thou make in the one curtain, and fifty loops shalt thou make in the edge of the curtain that is in the coupling of the second; that the loops may take hold one of another.

6 And thou shalt make fifty taches of gold, and couple the curtains together with the taches: and it shall be one tabernacle.

Exodus 36

8   And every wise hearted man among them that wrought the work of the tabernacle made ten curtains of fine twined linen, and blue, and purple, and scarlet: with cherubims of cunning work made he them.

9   The length of one curtain was twenty and eight cubits, and the breadth of one curtain four cubits: the curtains were all of one size.

10   And he coupled the five curtains one unto another: and the other five curtains he coupled one unto another.

11   And he made loops of blue on the edge of one curtain from the selvedge in the coupling: likewise he made in the uttermost side of another curtain, in the coupling of the second.

12   Fifty loops made he in one curtain, and fifty loops made he in the edge of the curtain which was in the coupling of the second: the loops held one curtain to another.

13   And he made fifty taches of gold, and coupled the curtains one unto another with the taches: so it became one tabernacle.

B. Goat Hair Covering

Exodus 26

7 And thou shalt make curtains of goats' hair to be a covering upon the tabernacle: eleven curtains shalt thou make.

8 The length of one curtain shall be thirty cubits, and the breadth of one curtain four cubits: and the eleven curtains shall be all of one measure.

9 And thou shalt couple five curtains by themselves, and six curtains by themselves, and shalt double the sixth curtain in the forefront of the tabernacle.

10 And thou shalt make fifty loops on the edge of the one curtain that is outmost in the coupling, and fifty loops in the edge of the curtain which coupleth the second.

11 And thou shalt make fifty taches of brass, and put the taches into the loops, and couple the tent together, that it may be one.

12 And the remnant that remaineth of the curtains of the tent, the half curtain that remaineth, shall hang over the backside of the tabernacle.

13 And a cubit on the one side, and a cubit on the other side of that which remaineth in the length of the curtains of the tent, it shall hang over the sides of the tabernacle on this side and on that side, to cover it.

Exodus 36

14   And he made curtains of goats' hair for the tent over the tabernacle: eleven curtains he made them.

15   The length of one curtain was thirty cubits, and four cubits was the breadth of one curtain: the eleven curtains were of one size.

16   And he coupled five curtains by themselves, and six curtains by themselves.

17   And he made fifty loops upon the uttermost edge of the curtain in the coupling, and fifty loops made he upon the edge of the curtain which coupleth the second.

18   And he made fifty taches of brass to couple the tent together, that it might be one.

C. Ram and Badger Skin Covering

Exodus 26
14   And thou shalt make a covering for the tent of rams' skins dyed red, and a covering above of badgers' skins.

Exodus 36
19   And he made a covering for the tent of rams' skins dyed red, and a covering of badgers' skins above that.

D. Hanging for the Door of the Tabernacle

Exodus 26

36 And thou shalt make an hanging for the door of the tent, of blue, and purple, and scarlet, and fine twined linen, wrought with needlework.

37 And thou shalt make for the hanging five pillars of shittim wood, and overlay them with gold, and their hooks shall be of gold: and thou shalt cast five sockets of brass for them.

Chapter 3 - Tabernacle Boards

Exodus 26

15 And thou shalt make boards for the tabernacle of shittim wood standing up.

16 Ten cubits shall be the length of a board, and a cubit and a half shall be the breadth of one board.

17 Two tenons shall there be in one board, set in order one against another: thus shalt thou make for all the boards of the tabernacle.

18 And thou shalt make the boards for the tabernacle, twenty boards on the south side southward.

19 And thou shalt make forty sockets of silver under the twenty boards; two sockets under one board for his two tenons, and two sockets under another board for his two tenons.

20 And for the second side of the tabernacle on the north side there shall be twenty boards:

21 And their forty sockets of silver; two sockets under one board, and two sockets under another board.

22 And for the sides of the tabernacle westward thou shalt make six boards.

23 And two boards shalt thou make for the corners of the tabernacle in the two sides.

24 And they shall be coupled together beneath, and they shall be coupled together above the head of it unto one ring: thus shall it be for them both; they shall be for the two corners.

25 And they shall be eight boards, and their sockets of silver, sixteen sockets; two sockets under one board, and two sockets under another board.

Exodus 36

20 And he made boards for the tabernacle of shittim wood, standing up.

The length of a board was ten cubits, and the breadth of a board one cubit and a half.

22 One board had two tenons, equally distant one from another: thus did he make for all the boards of the tabernacle.

23 And he made boards for the tabernacle; twenty boards for the south side southward:

24 And forty sockets of silver he made under the twenty boards; two sockets under

one board for his two tenons, and two sockets under another board for his two tenons.

25 And for the other side of the tabernacle, which is toward the north comer, he made twenty boards,

26 And their forty sockets of silver; two sockets under one board, and two sockets under another board.

27 And for the sides of the tabernacle westward he made six boards.

28 And two boards made he for the corners of the tabernacle in the two sides.

29 And they were coupled be-neath, and coupled together at the head thereof, to one ring: thus he did to both of them in both the corners.

30 And there were eight boards; and their sockets were sixteen sockets of silver, under every board two sockets.

Chapter 4 - Bars for the Tabernacle Boards

Exodus 26

26 And thou shalt make bars of shittim wood; five for the boards of the one side of the tabernacle,

27 And five bars for the boards of the other side of the tabernacle, and five bars for the boards of the side of the tabernacle, for the two sides westward.

28 And the middle bar in the midst of the boards shall reach from end to end.

29 And thou shalt overlay the boards with gold, and make their rings of gold for places for the bars: and thou shalt overlay the bars with gold.

30 And thou shalt rear up the tabernacle according to the fashion thereof which was shewed thee in the mount.

Exodus 36

31 And he made bars of shittim wood; five for the boards of the one side of the tabernacle,

32 And five bars for the boards of the other side of the tabernacle, and five bars for the boards of the tabernacle for the sides westward.

33 And he made the middle bar to shoot through the boards from the one end to the other.

34 And he overlaid the boards with gold, and made their rings of gold to be places for the bars, and overlaid the bars with gold.

Chapter 5 - Ark

Exodus 25

10 And they shall make an ark of shittim wood: two cubits and a half shall be the length thereof, and a cubit and a half the breadth thereof, and a cubit and a half the height thereof.

11 And thou shalt overlay it with pure gold, within and without shalt thou overlay it, and shalt make upon it a crown of gold round about.

12 And thou shalt cast four rings of gold for it, and put them in the four corners thereof; and two rings shall be in the one side of it, and two rings in the other side of it.

13 And thou shalt make staves of shittim wood, and overlay them with gold.

14 And thou shalt put the staves into the rings by the sides of the ark, that the ark may be borne with them.

15   The staves shall be in the rings of the ark: they shall not be taken from it.

And thou shalt put into the ark the testimony which I shall give thee.

Exodus 37

1   And Bezealeel made the ark of shittim wood: two cubits and a half was the length of it, and a cubit and a half the breadth of it, and a cubit and a half the height of it:

2   And he overlaid it with pure gold within and without, and made a crown of gold to it round about.

3   And he cast for it four rings of gold, to be set by the four corners of it; even two rings upon the one side of it and two rings upon the other side of it.

4   And he made staves of shittim wood, and overlaid them with gold.

5   And he put the staves into the rings by the sides of the ark, to bear the ark.

Chapter 6 - Mercy Seat

Exodus 25

17 And thou shalt make a mercy seat of pure gold: two cubits and a half shall be the length thereof, and a cubit and a half the breadth thereof.

18 And thou shalt make two cherubims of gold, of beaten work shalt thou make them, in the two ends of the mercy seat.

19 And make one cherub on the one end, and the other cherubims rub on the other end: even of the mercy seat shall ye make the cherubims on the two ends thereof.

20 And the cherubims shall stretch forth their wings on high, covering the mercy seat with their wings, and their faces shall look one to another; toward the mercy seat shall the faces of the cherubims be.

21 And thou shalt put the mercy seat above upon the ark; and in the ark thou shalt put the testimony that 1 shall give thee.

22 And there I will meet with thee, and I will commune with thee from above the mercy seat, from between the two cherubims which are upon the ark of the testimony, of all

things which I will give thee in commandment unto the children of Israel.

Exodus 37

6   And he made the mercy seat of pure gold: two cubits and a half was the length thereof, and one cubit and a half the breadth thereof.

7   And he made two cherubims of gold, beaten out of one piece made he them, on the two ends of the mercy seat;

8   One cherub on the end on this side, and another cherub on the other end on that side: out of the mercy seat made he the cherubims on the two ends thereof.

9   And the cherubims spread out their wings on high, and covered with their wings over the mercy seat, with their faces one to another; even to the mercy seatward were the faces of the cherubims.

Chapter 7 - Shewbread Table

Exodus 25

23 Thou shalt also make a table of shittim wood: two cubits shall be the length thereof, and a cubit the breadth thereof, and a cubit and a half the height thereof.

24 And thou shalt overlay it with pure gold, and make thereto a crown of gold round about.

25 And thou shalt make unto it a border of an hand breadth round about, and thou shalt make a golden crown to the border thereof round about.

26 And thou shalt make for it four rings of gold, and put the rings in the four corners that are on the four feet thereof.

27 Over against the border shall the rings be for places of the staves to bear the table.

28 And thou shalt make the staves of shittim wood, and overlay them with gold, that the table may be borne with them.

29 And thou shalt make the dishes thereof, and spoons thereof, and covers

thereof, and bowls thereof, to cover withal: of pure gold shalt thou make them.

And thou shalt set upon the table shewbread before me alway.

Exodus 37

10 And he made the table of shittim wood: two cubits was the length thereof, and a cubit the breadth thereof, and a cubit and a half the height thereof:

11 And he overlaid it with pure gold, and made thereunto a crown of gold round about.

12 Also he made thereunto a border of an handbreadth round about; and made a crown of gold for the border thereof round about.

13 And he cast for it four rings of gold, and put the rings upon the four corners that were in the four feet thereof.

14 Over against the border were the rings, the places for the staves to bear the table.

15 And he made the staves of shittim wood, and overlaid them with gold, to bear the table.

16 And he made the vessels which were upon the table, his dishes, and his spoons, and his bowls, and his covers to cover withal, of pure gold.

Leviticus 24

5   And thou shalt take fine flour, and bake twelve cakes thereof: two tenth deals shall be in one cake.

6   And thou shalt set them in two rows, six on a row, upon the pure table before the LORD.

7   And thou shalt put pure frankincense upon each row, that it may be on the bread for a memorial, even an offering made by fire unto the LORD.

8   Every sabbath he shall set it in order before the LORD continually, being taken from the children of Israel by an everlasting covenant.

9   And it shall be Aaron's and his sons'; and they shall eat it in the holy place: for it is most holy unto him of the offerings of the Lord made by fire by a perpetual statute.

Chapter 8 - Lamps

Exodus 25

31 And thou shalt make a candlestick of pure gold: of beaten work shall the candlestick be made: his shaft, and his branches, his bowls, his knops, and his flowers, shall be of the same.

32 And six branches shall come out of the sides of it; three branches of the candlestick out of the one side, and three branches of the candlestick out of the other side:

33 Three bowls made like unto almonds, with a knop and a flower in one branch; and three bowls made like almonds in the other branch, with a knop and a flower: so in the six branches that come out of the candlestick.

34 And in the candlestick shall be four bowls made like unto almonds, with their knops and their flowers.

35 And there shall be a knop under two branches of the same, and a knop under two branches of the same, and a knop under two branches of the same, according to the six branches that proceed out of the candlestick.

36 Their knops and their branches shall be of the same: all it shall be one beaten work of pure gold.

37 And thou shalt make the seven lamps thereof: and they shall light the lamps thereof, that they may give light over against it.

38 And the tongs thereof, and the snuffdishes thereof, shall be of pure gold.

39 Of a talent of pure gold shall he make it, with all these vessels.

40 And look that thou make them after their pattern, which was shewed thee in the mount.

Exodus 27

20 And thou shalt command the children of Israel, that they bring thee pure oil olive beaten for the light, to cause the lamp to burn always.

21 In the tabernacle of the congregation without the vail, which is before the testimony, Aaron and his sons shall order it from evening to morning before the Lord: it shall be a statute for ever unto their generations on the behalf of the children of Israel.

Exodus 37

And he made the candlestick of pure gold: of beaten work made he the candlestick; his shaft, and his branch, his bowls, his knops, and his flowers. were of the same:

18 And six branches going out of the sides thereof; three branches of the candlestick out of the one side thereof, and three branches of the candlestick out of the other side thereof:

19 Three bowls made after the fashion of almonds in one branch, a knop and a flower; and three bowls made like almonds in another branch, a knop and a flower: so throughout the six branches going out of the candlestick.

20 And in the candlestick were four bowls made like almonds, his knops, and his flowers:

21 And a knop under two branches of the same, and a knop under two branches of the same, and a knop under two branches of the same, according to the six branches going out of it.

22 Their knops and their branches were of the same: all of it was one beaten work of pure gold.

23 And he made his seven lamps, and his snuffers, and his snuffdishes, of pure gold.

24 Of a talent of pure gold made he it, and all the vessels thereof.

Leviticus 24

1   And the LORD spake unto Moses, saying,

2   Command the children of Israel, that they bring unto thee pure oil olive beaten for the light, to cause the lamps to burn continually.

3   Without the vail of the testimony, in the tabernacle of the congregation, shall Aaron order it from the evening unto the morning before the Lord continually : it shall be a statute for ever in your generations.

4   He shall order the lamps upon the pure candlestick before the LORD continually.

Numbers 8

1   And the LORD spake unto Moses, saying,

2   Speak unto Aaron, and say unto him, When thou lightest the lamps, the seven lamps shall give light over against the candlestick.

3   And Aaron did so; he lighted the lamps thereof over against the candlestick, as the LORD commanded Moses.

4   And this work of the candlestick was of beaten gold, unto the shaft thereof, unto the flowers thereof, was beaten work: according unto the pattern which the Lord had shewed Moses, so he made the candlestick.

The Hebrew Israelite Law Book

Chapter 9 - Vail

Exodus 26

31 And thou shalt make a vail of blue, and purple, and scarlet and fine twined linen of cunning work: with cherubims shall it be made:

32 And thou shalt hang it upon four pillars of shittim wood overlaid with gold: their hooks shall be of gold, upon the four sockets of silver.

33 And thou shalt hang up the vail under the taches, that thou mayest bring in thither within the vail the ark of the testimony: and the vail shall divide unto you between the holy place and the most holy.

34 And thou shalt put the mercy seat upon the ark of the testimony in the most holy place.

35 And thou shalt set the table without the vail, and the candlestick over against the table on the side of the tabernacle toward the south: and thou shalt put the table on the north side.

Exodus 36

35 And he made a vail of blue, and purple, and scarlet, and fine twined linen: with cherubims made he it of cunning work.

36 And he made thereunto four pillars of shittim wood, and overlaid them with gold: their hooks were of gold; and he cast for them four sockets of silver.

37 And he made an hanging for the tabernacle door of blue, and purple, and scarlet, and fine twined linen, of needlework;

38 And the five pillars of it with their hooks: and he overlaid their chapiters and their fillets with gold: but their five sockets were of brass

Chapter 10 – Altar of Earth

Exodus 20

24 An altar of earth thou shalt make unto me, and shalt sacrifice thereon thy burnt offerings, and thy peace offerings, thy sheep, and thine oxen: in all places where I record my name I will come unto thee, and I will bless thee.

25 And if thou wilt make me an altar of stone, thou shalt not build it of hewn stone: for if thou lift up thy tool upon it, thou hast polluted it.

26 Neither shalt thou go up by steps unto mine altar, that thy nakedness be not discovered thereon.

Chapter 11 – Altar of Shittim Wood

Exodus 27

1 And thou shalt make an altar of shittim wood, five cubits long, and five cubits broad; the altar shall be foursquare: and the height thereof shall be three cubits

2 And thou shalt make the horns of it upon the four corners thereof: his horns shall be of the same: and thou shalt overlay it with brass.

3 And thou shalt make his pans to receive his ashes, and his shovels, and his basons, and his fleshhooks, and his firepans: all the vessels thereof thou shalt make of brass.

4 And thou shalt make for it a grate of network of brass; and upon the net shalt thou make four brasen rings in the four corners thereof.

5 And thou shalt put it under the compass of the altar beneath, that the net may be even to the midst of the altar.

6 And thou shalt make staves for the altar, staves of shittim wood, and overlay them with brass.

7 And the staves shall be put into the rings, and the staves shall be upon the two sides of the altar, to bear it.

8 Hollow with boards shalt thou make it: as it was shewed thee in the mount, so shall they make it.

Exodus 38

1 And he made the altar of burnt offering of shittim wood: five cubits was the length thereof, and five cubits the breadth thereof; it was foursquare; and three cubits the height thereof.

2 And he made the horns thereof on the four corners of it; the horns thereof were of the same: and he overlaid it with brass.

3 And he made all the vessels of the altar, the pots, and the shovels, and the basons, and the fleshhooks, and the firepans: all the vessels thereof made he of brass.

4 And he made for the altar a brasen grate of network under the compass thereof beneath unto the midst of it.

5 And he cast four rings for the four ends of the grate of brass, to be places for the staves.

6   And he made the staves of shittim wood, and overlaid them with brass.

7   And he put the staves into the rings on the sides of the altar, to bear it withal; he made the altar hollow with boards.

Chapter 12 - Court of the Tabernacle

Exodus 27

9   And thou shalt make the court of the tabernacle: for the south side southward there shall be hangings for the court of fine twined linen of an hundred cubits long for one side:

10   And the twenty pillars thereof and their twenty sockets shall be of brass; the hooks of the pillars and their fillets shall be of silver.

11   And likewise for the north side in length there shall be hangings of an hundred cubits long, and his twenty pillars and then-twenty sockets of brass; the hooks of the pillars and their fillets of silver.

12   And for the breadth of the court on the west side shall be hangings of fifty cubits: their pillars ten, and their sockets ten.

13   And the breadth of the court on the east side eastward shall be fifty cubits.

14   The hangings of one side of the gate shall be fifteen cubits: their pillars three, and their sockets three.

15   And on the other side shall be hangings fifteen cubits: their pillars three, and their sockets three.

16   And for the gate of the court shall be an hanging of twenty cubits, of blue, and purple, and scarlet, and fine twined linen, wrought with needlework: and their pillars shall be four, and their sockets four.

17   All the pillars round about the court shall be filleted with silver; their hooks shall be of silver, and their sockets of brass.

18   The length of the court shall be an hundred cubits, and the breadth fifty every where, and the height five cubits of fine twined linen, and their sockets of brass.

Exodus 38

9   And he made the court: on the south side southward the hangings of the court were of fine twined linen, an hundred cubits:

10   Their pillars were twenty; and their brasen sockets twenty; the hooks of the pillars and their fillets were of silver.

11   And for the north side the hangings were an hundred cubits, their pillars were twenty, and their sockets of brass twenty; the hooks of the pillars and their fillets of silver.

12   And for the west side were hangings of fifty cubits, their pillars ten, and their sockets

ten; the hooks of the pillars and their fillets of silver.

13 And for the east side east-ward fifty cubits.

14 The hangings of the one side of the gate were fifteen cubits; their pillars three, and their sockets three.

15 And for the other side of the court gate, on this hand and that hand, were hangings of fifteen cubits; their pillars three, and their sockets three.

16 Ail the hangings of the court round about were of fine twined linen.

17 And the sockets for the pillars were of brass; the hooks of the pillars and their fillets of silver; and the overlaying of their chapiters of silver; and all the pillars of the court were filleted with silver.

18 And the hanging for the gate of the court was needlework, of blue, and purple, and scarlet, and fine twined linen: and twenty cubits was the length, and the height in the breadth was five cubits, answerable to the hangings of the court.

19 And their pillars were four, and their sockets of brass four; their hooks of silver, and the overlaying of their chapiters and their fillets of silver.

20 And all the pins of the tabernacle, and of the court round about, were of brass.

The Hebrew Israelite Law Book

The Hebrew Israelite Law Book

TITLE 17 – LEVITES AND PRIESTHOOD

Chapter 1 – Levites

A. Separating the Levites

Numbers 8

5 And the LORD spake unto Moses, saying,

6 Take the Levites from among the children of Israel, and cleanse them.

7 And thus shalt thou do unto them, to cleanse them: Sprinkle water of purifying upon them, and let them shave all their flesh, and let them wash their clothes, and so make themselves clean.

8 Then let them take a young bullock with his meat offering, even fine flour mingled with oil, and another young bullock shalt thou take for a sin offering.

9 And thou shalt bring the Levites before the tabernacle of the congregation: and thou shalt gather the whole assembly of the children of Israel together:

10 And thou shalt bring the Levites before the LORD: and the children of Israel shall put their hands upon the Levites:

11   And Aaron shall offer the Levites before the Lord for an offering of the children of Israel, that they may execute the service of the Lord.

12   And the Levites shall lay their hands upon the heads of the bullocks: and thou shalt offer the one for a sin offering, and the other for a burnt offering, unto the Lord, to make an atonement for the Levites.

13   And thou shalt set the Levites before Aaron, and before his sons, and offer them for an offering unto the LORD.

14   Thus shalt thou separate the Levites from among the children of Israel: and the Levites shall be mine.

15   And after that shall the Levites go in to do the service of the tabernacle of the congregation: and thou shalt cleanse them, and offer them for an offering.

16   For they are wholly given unto me from among the children of Israel; instead of such as open every womb, even instead of the firstborn of all the children of Israel, have I taken them unto me.

17   For all the firstborn of the children of Israel are mine, both man and beast: on the day that I smote every firstborn in the land of Egypt I sanctified them for myself.

18   And I have taken the Levites for all the firstborn of the children of Israel.

19 And I have given the Levites as a gift to Aaron and to his sons from among the children of Israel, to do the service of the children of Israel in the tabernacle of the congregation, and to make an atonement for the children of Israel: that there be no plague among the children of Israel, when the children of Israel come nigh unto the sanctuary.

20 And Moses, and Aaron, and all the congregation of the children of Israel, did to the Levites according unto all that the LORD commanded Moses concerning the Levites, so did the children of Israel unto them.

21 And the Levites were purified, and they washed their

clothes; and Aaron offered them as an offering before the LORD; and Aaron made an atonement for them to cleanse them.

22 And after that went the Levites in to do their service in the tabernacle of the congregation before Aaron, and before his sons: as the LORD had commanded Moses concerning the Levites, so did they unto them.

23 And the LORD spake unto Moses, saying,

24 This is it that belongeth unto the Levites: from twenty and five years old and

upward they shall go in to wait upon the service of the tabernacle of the congregation:

25 And from the age of fifty years they shall cease waiting upon the service thereof and shall serve no more:

26 But shall minister with their brethren in the tabernacle of the congregation, to keep the charge, and shall do no service. Thus shalt thou do unto the Levites touching their charge.

B. The Tithe

Leviticus 27

30 And all the tithe of the land, whether of the seed of the land, or of the fruit of the tree, is the LORD'S: it is holy unto the LORD.

31 And if a man will at all redeem ought of his tithes, he shall add thereto the fifth part thereof.

32 And concerning the tithe of the herd, or of the flock, even of whatsoever passeth under the rod, the tenth shall be holy unto the LORD.

33 He shall not search whether it be good or bad, neither shall he change it: and if he change it at all, then both it and the change thereof shall be holy; it shall not be redeemed.

34 These are the commandments, which the LORD commanded Moses for the children of Israel in mount Sinai.

Numbers 18

20 And the LORD spake unto Aaron, Thou shalt have no inheritance in their land, neither shalt thou have any part among them: I am thy part and thine inheritance among the children of Israel.

21 And, behold, I have given the children of Levi all the tenth in Israel for an inheritance, for their service which they serve, even the service of the tabernacle of the congregation.

22 Neither must the children of Israel henceforth come nigh the tabernacle of the congregation, lest they bear sin, and die.

23 But the Levites shall do the service of the tabernacle of the congregation, and they shall bear their iniquity: it shall be a statute for ever throughout your generations, that among the children of Israel they have no inheritance.

24 But the tithes of the children of Israel, which they offer as an heave offering unto the LORD, I have given to the Levites to inherit: therefore I have said unto them, Among the children of Israel they shall have no inheritance.

Deuteronomy 14

22 Thou shalt truly tithe all the increase of thy seed, that the field bringeth forth year by year.

23 And thou shalt eat before the LORD thy God, in the place which he shall choose to place his name there, the tithe of thy corn, of thy wine, and of thine oil, and the firstlings of thy herds and of thy flocks; that thou mayest learn to fear the LORD thy God always.

24 And if the way be too long for thee, so that thou art not able to carry it; or if the place be too far from thee, which the LORD thy God shall choose to set his name there, when the LORD thy God hath blessed thee:

25 Then shalt thou turn it into money, and bind up the money in thine hand, and shalt go unto the place which the LORD thy God shall choose:

26 And thou shalt bestow that money for whatsoever thy soul lusteth after, for oxen, or for sheep, or for wine, or for strong drink, or for whatsoever thy soul desireth: and thou shalt eat there before the LORD thy God, and thou shalt rejoice, thou, and thine household,

27 And the Levite that is within thy gates; thou shalt not forsake him; for he hath no part nor inheritance with thee.

28 At the end of three years thou shalt bring forth all the tithe of thine increase the same year, and shalt lay it up within thy gates:

29 And the Levite, (because he hath no part nor inheritance with thee,) and the stranger, and the fatherless, and the widow, which are within thy gates, shall come, and shall eat and be satisfied; that the LORD thy God may bless thee in all the work of thine hand which thou doest.

Deuteronomy 26

12 When thou hast made an end of tithing all the tithes of thine increase the third year, which is the year of tithing, and hast given it unto the Levite, the stranger, the fatherless, and the widow, that they may eat within thy gates, and be filled;

13 Then thou shalt say before the LORD thy God, I have brought away the hallowed things out of mine house, and also have given them unto the Levite, and unto the stranger, to the fatherless, and to the widow, according to all thy commandments which thou hast commanded me: I have not transgressed thy commandments, neither have I forgotten them:

14 I have not eaten thereof in my mourning, neither have I taken away ought thereof for any unclean use, nor given ought

thereof for the dead: but I have hearkened to the voice of the LORD my God, and have done according to all that thou hast commanded me.

C. Heave Offering of the Tithe

Numbers 18

25 And the LORD spake unto Moses, saying,

26 Thus speak unto the Levites, and say unto them, When ye take of the children of Israel the tithes which I have given you from them for your inheritance, then ye shall offer up an heave offering of it for the LORD, even a tenth part of the tithe.

27 And this your heave offering shall be reckoned unto you, as though it were the corn of the threshingfloor, and as the fulness of the winepress.

28 Thus ye also shall offer an heave offering unto the LORD of all your tithes, which ye receive of the children of Israel; and ye shall give thereof the LORD'S heave offering to Aaron the priest.

29 Out of all your gifts ye shall offer every heave offering of the LORD, of all the best thereof, even the hallowed part thereof out of it.

30 Therefore thou shalt say unto them, When ye have heaved the best thereof from it, then it shall be counted unto the Levites as the increase of the threshingfloor, and as the increase of the winepress.

31 And ye shall eat it in every place, ye and your households: for it is your reward for your service in the tabernacle of the congregation.

32 And ye shall bear no sin by reason of it, when ye have heaved from it the best of it: neither shall ye pollute the holy things of the children of Israel, lest ye die.

D. Levite Inheritance

Numbers 35

1 And the LORD spake unto Moses in the plains of Moab by Jordan near Jericho, saying,

2 Command the children of Israel, that they give unto the Levites of the inheritance of their possession cities to dwell in; and ye shall give also unto the Levites suburbs for the cities round about them.

3 And the cities shall they have to dwell in; and the suburbs of them shall be for their cattle, and for their goods, and for all their beasts.

4 And the suburbs of the cities, which ye shall give unto the Levites, shall reach from

the wall of the city and outward a thousand cubits round about.

5   And ye shall measure from without the city on the east side two thousand cubits, and on the south side two thousand cubits, and on the west side two thousand cubits, and on the north side two thousand cubits; and

the city shall be in the midst: this shall be to them the suburbs

of the cities.

6   And among the cities which ye shall give unto the Levites there shall be six cities for refuge, which ye shall appoint for the manslayer, that he may flee thither: and to them ye shall add forty and two cities.

7   So all the cities which ye shall give to the Levites shall be forty and eight cities: them shall ye give with their suburbs.

8   And the cities which ye shall give shall be of the possession of the children of Israel: from them that have many ye shall give many; but from them that have few ye shall give few: every one shall give of his cities unto the Levites according to his inheritance which he inheriteth.

Deuteronomy 18
1   The priests the Levites, and all the tribe of Levi, shall have no part nor inheritance

with Israel: they shall eat the offerings of the LORD made by

fire, and his inheritance.

2   Therefore   shall   they   have   no inheritance among their brethren : the LORD is their inheritance, as he hath said unto them.

3   And this shall be the priest's due from the people, from them that offer a sacrifice, whether it be ox or sheep; and they shall give unto the priest the shoulder, and the two cheeks, and the maw.

4   The firstfruit also of thy corn, of thy wine, and of thine oil, and the first of the fleece of thy sheep, shalt thou give him.

5   For the LORD thy God hath chosen him out of all thy tribes, to stand to minister in the name of the LORD, him and his sons for ever.

6   And if a Levite come from any of thy gates out of all Israel, where he sojourned, and come with all the desire of his mind unto the place which the LORD shall choose;

7   Then he shall minister in the name of the LORD his God, as all his brethren the Levites do, which stand there before the LORD.

8   They shall have like portions to eat, beside that which cometh of the sale of his patrimony.

9   If When thou art come into the land which the LORD thy God giveth thee, thou shalt not learn to do after the abominations of those nations.

Chapter 2 - Aaron and Sons as Priests

Numbers 17

1   And the LORD spake unto Moses, saying,

2   Speak unto the children of Israel, and take of every one of them a rod according to the house of their fathers, of all their princes according to the house of their fathers twelve rods: write thou every man's name upon his rod.

3   And thou shalt write Aaron's name upon the rod of Levi: for one rod shall be for the head of the house of their fathers.

4 And thou shalt lay them up in the tabernacle of the congregation before the testimony, where I will meet with you.

5 And it shall come to pass, that the man's rod, whom I shall choose, shall blossom: and I will make to cease from me the murmurings of the children of Israel, whereby they murmur against you.

6 And Moses spake unto the children of Israel, and every one of their princes gave him a rod apiece, for each prince one, according to their fathers' houses, even twelve rods: and the rod of Aaron was among their rods.

7 And Moses laid up the rods before the LORD in the tabernacle of witness.

8 And it came to pass, that on the morrow Moses went into the tabernacle of witness; and, behold, the rod of Aaron for the house of Levi was budded, and brought forth buds, and bloomed blossoms, and yielded almonds.

9 And Moses brought out all the rods from before the LORD unto all the children of Israel: and they looked, and took every man his rod.

10 And the LORD said unto Moses, Bring Aaron's rod again before the testimony, to be kept for a token against the rebels; and thou shalt quite take away their murmurings from me, that they die not.

11 And Moses did so: as the LORD commanded him, so did he.

Exodus 28
1   And take thou unto thee Aaron thy brother, and his sons with him, from among the children of Israel, that he may minister unto me in the priest's office, even Aaron, Nadab and Abihu, Eleazar and Ithamar, Aaron's sons.

Exodus 39
27 And they made coats of fine linen of woven work for Aaron, and for his sons,
28 And a mitre of fine linen, and goodly bonnets of fine linen, and linen breeches of fine twined linen,
29 And a girdle of fine twined linen, and blue, and purple, and scarlet, of needlework; as the Lord commanded Moses.

Numbers 18
1   And the LORD said unto Aaron, Thou and thy sons and thy father's house with thee shall bear the iniquity of the sanctuary: and thou and thy sons with thee shall bear the iniquity of your priesthood.
2   And thy brethren also of the tribe of Levi, the tribe of thy father, bring thou with thee, that they may be joined unto thee, and

minister unto thee: but thou and thy sons with thee shall minister before the tabernacle of witness.

3   And they shall keep thy charge, and the charge of all the tabernacle: only they shall not come nigh the vessels of the sanctuary and the altar, that neither they, nor ye also, die.

4   And they shall be joined unto thee, and keep the charge of the tabernacle of the congregation, for all the service of the tabernacle: and a stranger shall not come nigh unto you.

5   And ye shall keep the charge of the sanctuary, and the charge of the altar: that there be no wrath any more upon the children of Israel.

6   And I, behold, I have taken your brethren the Levites from among the children of Israel: to you they are given as a gift for the LORD, to do the service of the tabernacle of the congregation.

7   Therefore thou and thy sons with thee shall keep your priest's office for every thing of the altar, and within the vail; and ye shall serve: I have given your priest's office unto you as a service of gift: and the stranger that cometh nigh shall be put to death.

Numbers 25

10 And the LORD spake unto Moses, saying,

11 Phinehas, the son of Eleazar, the son of Aaron the priest, hath turned my wrath away from the children of Israel, while he was zealous for my sake among them, that I consumed not the children of Israel in my jealousy.

12 Wherefore say, Behold, I give unto him my covenant of peace:

13 And he shall have it, and his seed after him, even the covenant of an everlasting priesthood; because he was zealous for his God, and made an atonement for the children of Israel.

A. Defiled for the Dead

Leviticus 21

1 And the LORD said unto Moses, Speak unto the priests the sons of Aaron, and say unto them, There shall none be defiled for the dead among his people:

2 But for his kin, that is near unto him, that is, for his mother, and for his father, and for his son, and for his daughter, and for his brother,

3 And for his sister a virgin, that is nigh unto him, which hath had no husband; for her may he be defiled.

4   But he shall not defile himself, being a chief man among his people, to profane himself.

B. Baldness

Leviticus 21

5   They shall not make baldness upon their head, neither shall they shave off the corner of their beard, nor make any cuttings in their flesh.

6   They shall be holy unto their God, and not profane the name of their God: for the offerings of the LORD made by fire, and the bread of their God, they do offer: therefore they shall be holy.

C. Marriage

Leviticus 21

7   They shall not take a wife that is a whore, or profane; neither shall they take a woman put away from her husband: for he is holy unto his God.

8   Thou shalt sanctify him therefore; for he offereth the bread of thy God: he shall be holy unto thee: for I the LORD, which sanctify you, am holy.

D. Daughter

Leviticus 21
8   And the daughter of any priest, if she profane herself by playing the whore, she profaneth her father: she shall be burnt with fire.

E. Wine and Strong Drink

Leviticus 10
8   And the LORD spake unto Aaron, saying,
9   Do not drink wine nor strong drink, thou, nor thy sons with thee, when ye go into the tabernacle of the congregation, lest ye die: it shall be a statute for ever throughout your generations:
10   And that ye may put difference between holy and unholy, and between unclean and clean;
11   And that ye may teach the children of Israel all the statutes which the LORD hath spoken unto them by the hand of Moses.

F. Blemish

Leviticus 21

16 And the LORD spake unto Moses, saying,

17 Speak unto Aaron, saying, Whosoever he be of thy seed in their generations that hath any blemish, let him not approach to offer the bread of his God.

18 For whatsoever man he be that hath a blemish, he shall not approach: a blind man, or a lame, or he that hath a flat nose, or any thing superfluous,

19 Or a man that is broken-footed, or brokenhanded,

20 Or crookbackt, or a dwarf, or that hath a blemish in his eye, or be scurvy, or scabbed, or hath his stones broken;

21 No man that hath a blemish of the seed of Aaron the priest shall come nigh to offer the offerings of the LORD made by fire: he hath a blemish; he shall not come nigh to offer the bread of his God.

22 He shall eat the bread of his God, both of the most holy, and of the holy.

23 Only he shall not go in unto the vail, nor come nigh unto the altar, because he hath a blemish; that he profane not my sanctuaries: for I the LORD do sanctify them.

24 And Moses told it unto Aaron, and to his sons, and unto all the children of Israel.

G. Cleanliness

Leviticus 22

1 And the LORD spake unto Moses, saying,

2 Speak unto Aaron and to his sons, that they separate themselves from the holy things of the children of Israel, and that they profane not my holy name in those things which they hallow unto me: I am the LORD.

3 Say unto them, Whosoever he be of all your seed among your generations, that goeth unto the holy things, which the children of Israel hallow unto the LORD, having his uncleanness upon him, that soul shall be cut off from my presence: I am the LORD.

4 What man soever of the seed of Aaron is a leper, or hath a running issue; he shall not eat of the holy things, until he be clean. And whoso toucheth any thing that is unclean by the dead, or a man whose seed goeth from him;

5 Or whosoever toucheth any creeping thing, whereby he may be made unclean, or a man of whom he may take uncleanness, whatsoever uncleanness he hath;

6 The soul which hath touched any such shall be unclean until even, and shall not eat of the holy things, unless he wash his flesh with water.

7   And when the sun is down, he shall be clean, and shall afterward eat of the holy things; because it is his food.

8   That which dieth of itself, or is torn with beasts, he shall not eat to defile himself therewith: I am the LORD.

9   They shall therefore keep mine ordinance, lest they bear sin for it, and die therefore, if they profane it: I the LORD do sanctify them.

H. Eating the Holy Things

Leviticus 22

10 There shall no stranger eat of the holy thing: a sojourner of the priest, or an hired servant, shall not eat of the holy thing.

11 But if the priest buy any soul with his money, he shall eat of it, and he that is born in his house: they shall eat of his meat.

12 If the priest's daughter also be married unto a stranger, she may not eat of an offering of the holy things.

13 But if the priest's daughter be a widow, or divorced, and have no child, and is returned unto her father's house, as in her youth, she shall eat of her father's meat: but there shall no stranger eat thereof.

14 And if a man eat of the holy thing unwittingly, then he shall put the fifth part

thereof unto it, and shall give it unto the priest with the holy thing.

15 And they shall not profane the holy things of the children of Israel, which they offer unto the LORD;

16 Or suffer them to bear the iniquity of trespass, when they eat their holy things: for I the LORD do sanctify them.

I. High Priest

a. Uncovering His Head and Rending His Clothes

Leviticus 21

10 And he that is the high priest among his brethren, upon whose head the anointing oil was poured, and that is consecrated to put on the garments, shall not uncover his head, nor rend his clothes;

b. Defile Himself and Leave the Sanctuary

Leviticus 21

11 Neither shall he go in to any dead body, nor defile himself for his father, or for his mother;

12 Neither shall he go out of the sanctuary, nor profane the sanctuary of his

God; for the crown of the anointing oil of his God is upon him: I am the LORD.

c. Marriage

Leviticus 21

13　And he shall take a wife in her virginity.

14　A widow, or a divorced woman, or profane, or an harlot, these shall he not take: but he shall take a virgin of his own people to wife.

15　Neither shall he profane his seed among his people: for I the LORD do sanctify him.

J. Aaron's Garment (High Priest)

Exodus 28

2　And thou shalt make holy garments for Aaron thy brother for glory and for beauty.

3　And thou shalt speak unto all that are wise hearted, whom I have filled with the spirit of wisdom, that they may make Aaron's garments to consecrate him, that he may minister unto me in the priest's office.

4　And these are the garments which they shall make; a breastplate, and an ephod, and a robe, and a broidered coat, a mitre, and a girdle: and they shall make holy garments for

Aaron thy brother, and his sons, that he may minister unto me in the priest's office.

5   And they shall take gold, and blue, and purple, and scarlet, and fine linen.

Exodus 28

39 And thou shalt embroider the coat of fine linen, and thou shalt make the mitre of fine linen, and thou shalt make the girdle of needlework.

Exodus 28

29 And the holy garments of Aaron shall be his sons' after him, to be anointed therein, and to be consecrated in them.

30 And that son that is priest in his stead shall put them on seven days, when he cometh   into   the   tabernacle   of   the congregation to minister in the holy place.

a. Ephod

Exodus 28

6   And they shall make the ephod of gold, of blue, and of purple, of scarlet, and fine twined linen, with running work.

7   It shall have the two shoulderpieces thereof joined at the two edges thereof; and so it shall be joined together.

Exodus 28

9 And thou shalt take two onyx stones, and grave on them the names of the Children of Israel:

10 Six of their names on one stone, and the other six names of the rest on the other stone, according to their birth.

11 With the work of an engraver in stone, like the engravings of a signet, shalt thou engrave the two stones with the names of the children of Israel: thou shalt make them to be set in ouches of gold.

12 And thou shalt put the two stones upon the shoulders of the ephod for stones of memorial unto the children of Israel: and Aaron shall bear their names before the LORD upon his two shoulders for a memorial.

Exodus 39

2 And he made the ephod of gold, blue, and purple, and scarlet, and fine twined linen.

3 And they did beat the gold into thin plates, and cut it into wires, to work it in the blue, and in the purple, and in the scarlet, and in the fine linen, with cunning work.

4 They made shoulderpieces for it, to couple it together: by the two edges was it coupled together.

Exodus 39

6   And they wrought onyx stones inclosed in ouches of gold, graven, as signets are graven, with the names of the children of Israel.

7   And he put them on the shoulders of the ephod, that they should be stones for a memorial to the children of Israel; as the LORD commanded Moses.

b. Girdle

Exodus 28

8   And the curious girdle of the ephod, which is upon it, shall be of the same, according to the work thereof; even of gold, of blue, and purple, and scarlet, and fine twined linen.

Exodus 39

5   And the curious girdle of his e -phod, that was upon it, was of the same, according to the work thereof; of gold, blue, and purple, and scarlet, and fine twined linen; as the Lord commanded Moses.

c. Breastplate

Exodus 28

13   And thou shalt make ouches of gold;

14 And two chains of pure gold at the ends; of wreathen work shalt thou make them, and fasten the wreathen chains to the ouches.

15 And thou shalt make the breastplate of judgment with cunning work; after the work of the ephod thou shalt make it; of gold, of blue, and of purple, and of scarlet, and of fine twined linen, shalt thou make it.

16 Foursquare it shall be being doubled; a span shall be the length thereof, and a span shall be the breadth thereof.

17 And thou shalt set in it settings of stones, even four rows of stones: the first row shall be a sardius, a topaz, and a carbuncle: this shall be the first row.

18 And the second row shall be an emerald, a sapphire, and a diamond.

19 And the third row a ligure, an agate, and an amethyst.

20 And the fourth row a beryl, and an onyx, and a jasper: they shall be set in gold in their inclosings.

21 And the stones shall be with the names of the children of Israel, twelve, according to their names, like the engravings of a signet; every one with his name shall they be according to the twelve tribes.

Exodus 28

29 And Aaron shall bear the names of the children of Israel in the breastplate of judgment upon his heart, when he goeth in unto the holy place, for a memorial before the LORD continually.

30 And thou shalt put in the breastplate of judgment the Urim and the Thummim; and they shall be upon Aaron's heart, when he goeth in before the LORD : and Aaron shall bear the judgment of the children of Israel upon his heart before the LORD continually.

Exodus 39

8   And he made the breastplate of cunning work, like the work of the ephod; of gold, blue, and purple, and scarlet, and fine twined linen.

9   It was foursquare; they made the breastplate double: a span was the length thereof, and a span the breadth thereof, being doubled.

10 And they set in it four rows of stones: the first row was a sardius, a topaz, and a carbuncle: this was the first row.

11 And the second row, an emerald, a sapphire, and a diamond.

12 And the third row, a ligure, an agate, and an amethyst

13 And the fourth row, a beryl, an onyx, and a jasper: they were inclosed in ouches of gold in their inclosings.

14 And the stones were according to the names of the children of Israel, twelve, according to their names, like the engravings of a signet, every one with his name, according to the twelve tribes.

d. Broidered Coat

Exodus 28
22 And thou shalt make upon the breastplate chains at the ends of wreathen work of pure gold.

23 And thou shalt make upon the breastplate two rings of gold, and shalt put the two rings on the two ends of the breastplate.

24 And thou shalt put the two wreathen chains of gold in the two rings which are on the ends of the breastplate.

25 And the other two ends of the two wreathen chains thou shalt fasten in the two ouches, and put them on the shoulderpieces of the ephod before it.

26 And thou shalt make two rings of gold, and thou shalt put them upon the two ends of the breastplate in the border thereof, which is in the side of the ephod inward.

27 And two other rings of gold thou shalt make, and shalt put them on the two sides of the ephod underneath, toward the forepart thereof, over against the other coupling thereof, above the curious girdle of the ephod.

28 And they shall bind the breastplate by the rings thereof unto the rings of the ephod with a lace of blue, that it may be above the curious girdle of the ephod, and that the breastplate be not loosed from the ephod.

Exodus 39

15 And they made upon the breastplate chains at the ends, of wreathen work of pure gold.

16 And they made two ouches of gold, and two gold rings; and put the two rings in the two ends of the breastplate.

17 And they put the two wreathen chains of gold in the two rings on the ends of the breastplate.

18 And the two ends of the two wreathen chains they fastened in the two ouches, and put them on the shoulderpieces of the ephod, before it.

19 And they made two rings of gold, and put them on the two ends of the breastplate, upon the border of it, which was on the side of the ephod inward.

20 And they made two other golden rings, and put them on the two sides of the ephod underneath, toward the forepart of it, over against the other coupling thereof, above the curious girdle of the ephod.

21 And they did bind the breastplate by his rings unto the rings of the ephod with a lace of blue, that it might be above the curious girdle of the ephod, and that the breastplate might not be loosed from the ephod; as the LORD commanded Moses.

e. Robe

Exodus 28

31 And thou shalt make the robe of the ephod all of blue.

32 And there shall be an hole in the top of it, in the midst thereof: it shall have a binding of woven work round about the hole of it, as it were the hole of an habergeon, that it be not rent.

33 And beneath upon the hem of it thou shalt make pomegranates of blue, and of purple, and of scarlet, round about the hem thereof; and bells of gold between them round about:

34 A golden bell and a pomegranate, a golden bell and a pomegranate, upon the hem of the robe round about.

35 And it shall be upon Aaron to minister: and his sound shall be heard when he goeth in unto the holy place before the LORD, and when he cometh out, that he die not.

Exodus 39
22 And he made the robe of the ephod of woven work, all of blue.

23 And there was an hole in the midst of the robe, as the hole of an habergeon, with a band round about the hole, that it should not rend.

24 And they made upon the hems of the robe pomegranates of blue, and purple, and scarlet, and twined linen.

25 And they made bells of pure gold, and put the bells between the pomegranates upon the hem of the robe, round about between the pomegranates;

26 A bell and a pomegranate, a bell and a pomegranate, round about the hem of the robe to minister in; as the Lord commanded Moses.

f. Mitre

Exodus 28
36 And thou shalt make a plate of pure gold, and grave upon it, like the engravings of a signet, HOLINESS TO THE LORD.

37 And thou shalt put it on a blue lace, that it may be upon the mitre; upon the forefront of the mitre it shall be.

38 And it shall be upon Aaron's forehead, that Aaron may bear the iniquity of the holy things, which the Children of Israel shall hallow in all their holy gifts; and it shall be always upon his forehead, that they may be accepted before the LORD.

Exodus 39

30 And they made the plate of the holy crown of pure gold, and wrote upon it a writing, like to the engravings of a signet, HOLINESS TO THE LORD.

31 And they tied unto it a lace of blue, to fasten it on high upon the mitre; as the LORD commanded Moses.

32 Thus was all the work of the tabernacle of the tent of the congregation finished: and the children of Israel did according to all that the LORD commanded Moses, so did they.

K. Aaron's Sons Garments (Priest's)

Exodus 28

40 And for Aaron's sons thou shalt make coats, and thou shalt make for them girdles,

and bonnets shalt thou make for them, for glory and for beauty.

41　And thou shalt put them upon Aaron thy brother, and his sons with him; and shalt anoint them, and consecrate them, and sanctify them, that they may minister unto me in the priest's office.

42 And thou shalt make them linen breeches to cover their nakedness; from the loins even unto the thighs they shall reach:

43 And they shall be upon Aaron, and upon his sons, when they come in unto the tabernacle of the congregation, or when they come near unto the altar to minister in the holy place; that they bear not iniquity, and die: it shall be a statute for ever unto him and his seed after him.

L. Hallowing the Priests

Exodus 29
And this is the thing that thou shalt do unto them to hallow them, to minister unto me in the priest's office: Take one young bullock, and two rams without blemish,

2　And unleavened bread, and cakes unleavened tempered with oil, and wafers unleavened anointed with oil: of wheaten flour shalt thou make them.

3   And thou shalt put them into one basket, and bring them in the basket, with the bullock and the two rams.

4   And Aaron and his sons thou shalt bring unto the door of the tabernacle of the congregation, and shalt wash them with water.

5   And thou shalt take the garments, and put upon Aaron the coat, and the robe of the ephod, and the ephod, and the breastplate, and gird him with the curious girdle of the ephod:

6   And thou shalt put the mitre upon his head, and put the holy crown upon the mitre.

7   Then shalt thou take the anointing oil, and pour it upon his head, and anoint him.

8   And thou shalt bring his sons, and put coats upon them.

9   And thou shalt gird them with girdles, Aaron and his sons, and put the bonnets on them: and the priest's office shall be theirs for a perpetual statute: and thou shalt consecrate Aaron and his sons.

Exodus 29
33 And they shall eat those things wherewith the atonement was made, to consecrate and to sanctify them: but a stranger shall not eat thereof because they are holy.

34 And if ought of the flesh of the consecrations, or of the bread, remain unto the morning, then thou shalt burn the remainder with fire: it shall not be eaten, because it is holy.

a. Bullock

Exodus 29
10 And thou shalt cause a bullock to be brought before the tabernacle of the congregation: and Aaron and his sons shall put their hands upon the head of the bullock.

11 And thou shalt kill the bullock before the LORD, by the door of the tabernacle of the congregation.

12 And thou shalt take of the blood of the bullock, and put it upon the horns of the altar with thy finger, and pour all the blood beside the bottom of the altar.

13 And thou shalt take all the fat that covereth the inwards, and the caul that is above the liver, and the two kidneys, and the fat that is upon them, and burn them upon the altar.

14 But the flesh of the bullock, and his skin, and his dung, shalt thou burn with fire without the camp: it is a sin offering.

b. Rams

Exodus 29

15 Thou shalt also take one ram; and Aaron and his sons shall put their hands upon the head of the ram.

16 And thou shalt slay the ram, and thou shalt take his blood, and sprinkle it round about upon the altar.

17 And thou shalt cut the ram in pieces, and wash the inwards of him, and his legs, and put them unto his pieces, and unto his head.

18 And thou shalt burn the whole ram upon the altar: it is a burnt offering unto the LORD: it is a sweet savour, an offering made by fire unto the LORD.

19 And thou shalt take the other ram; and Aaron and his sons shall put their hands upon the head of the ram.

20 Then shalt thou kill the ram, and take of his blood, and put it upon the tip of the right ear of Aaron, and upon the tip of the right ear of his sons, and upon the thumb of their right hand, and upon the great toe of their right foot, and sprinkle the blood upon the altar round about.

21 And thou shalt take of the blood that is upon the altar, and of the anointing oil, and sprinkle it upon Aaron, and upon his

garments, and upon his sons, and upon the garments of his sons with him: and he shall be hallowed, and his garments, and his sons, and his sons' garments with him.

22 Also thou shalt take of the ram the fat and the rump, and the fat that covereth the inwards, and the caul above the liver, and the two kidneys, and the fat that is upon them, and the right shoulder; for it is a ram of consecration:

Exodus 29

26 And thou shalt take the breast of the ram of Aaron's consecration, and wave it for a wave offering before the LORD: and it shall be thy part.

27 And thou shalt sanctify the breast of the wave offering, and the shoulder of the heave offering, which is waved, and which is heaved up, of the ram of the consecration, even of that which is for Aaron, and of that which is for his sons:

28 And it shall be Aaron's and his sons' by a statute for ever from the children of Israel: for it is an heave offering: and it shall be an heave offering from the children of Israel of the sacrifice of their peace offerings, even their heave offering unto the LORD.

Exodus 29

31 And thou shalt take the ram of the consecration, and seethe his flesh in the holy place.

32 And Aaron and his sons shall eat the flesh of the ram, and the bread that is in the basket, by the door of the tabernacle of the congregation.

c. Bread

Exodus 29

23 And one loaf of bread, and one cake of oiled bread, and one wafer out of the basket of the unleavened bread that is before the LORD:

24 And thou shalt put all in the hands of Aaron, and in the hands of his sons; and shalt wave them for a wave offering before the LORD.

25 And thou shalt receive them of then hands, and burn them upon the altar for a burnt offering, for a sweet savour before the LORD: it is an offering made by fire unto the LORD.

d. Priest Seven Day Consecration

Exodus 29

35 And thus shalt thou do unto Aaron, and to his sons, according to all things which I

have commanded thee: seven days shalt thou consecrate them.

36 And thou shalt offer every day a bullock for a sin offering for atonement: and thou shalt cleanse the altar, when thou hast made an atonement for it, and thou shalt anoint it, to sanctify it.

37 Seven days thou shalt make an atonement for the altar, and sanctify it; and it shall be an altar most holy: whatsoever toucheth the altar shall be holy.

38 Now this is that which thou shalt offer upon the altar; two lambs of the first year day by day continually.

39 The one lamb thou shalt offer in the morning; and the other lamb thou shalt offer at even:

40 And with the one lamb a tenth deal of flour mingled with the fourth part of an hin of beaten oil; and the fourth part of an hin of wine for a drink offering.

41 And the other lamb thou shalt offer at even, and shalt do thereto according to the meat offering of the morning, and according to the drink offering thereof, for a sweet savour, an offering made by fire unto the LORD.

42 This shall be a continual burnt offering throughout your generations at the door of the tabernacle of the congregation before the

LORD: where I will meet you, to speak there unto thee.

43 And there I will meet with the children of Israel, and the tabernacle shall be sanctified by my glory.

44 And I will sanctify the tabernacle of the congregation, and the altar: I will sanctify also both Aaron and his sons, to minister to me in the priest's office.

45 And I will dwell among the children of Israel, and will be their God.

46 And they shall know that I am the LORD their God, that brought them forth out of the land of Egypt, that I may dwell among them: I am the LORD their God.

M. Incense Altar

Exodus 30

1 And thou shalt make an altar to burn incense upon: of shittim wood shalt thou make it.

2 A cubit shall be the length thereof, and a cubit the breadth thereof; foursquare shall it be: and two cubits shall be the height thereof: the horns therof shall be of the same.

3 And thou shalt overlay it with pure gold, the top thereof, and the sides thereof round about, and the horns thereof; and thou shalt make unto it a crown of gold round about.

4   And two golden rings shalt thou make to it under the crown of it, by the two corners thereof, upon the two sides of it shalt thou make it; and they shall be for places for the staves to bear it withal.

5   And thou shalt make the staves of shittim wood, and overlay them with gold.

6   And thou shalt put it before the vail that is by the ark of the testimony, before the mercy seat that is over the testimony, where I will meet with thee.

7   And Aaron shall burn thereon sweet incense every morning: when he dresseth the lamps, he shall burn incense upon it.

8   And when Aaron lighteth the lamps at even, he shall burn incense upon it, a perpetual in-cense before the LORD throughout your generations.

9   Ye shall offer no strange incense thereon, nor burnt sacrifice, nor meat offering; neither shall ye pour drink offering thereon.

10 And Aaron shall make an atonement upon the horns of it once in a year with the blood of the sin offering of atonements: once in the year shall he make atonement upon it throughout your generations: it is most holy unto the LORD.

Exodus 37

25 And he made the incense altar of shittim wood: the length of it was a cubit, and the breadth of it a cubit; it was foursquare; and two cubits was the height of it; the horns thereof were of the same.

26 And he overlaid it with pure gold, both the top of it, and the sides thereof round about, and the horns of it: also he made unto it a crown of gold round about.

27 And he made two rings of gold for it under the crown thereof, by the two corners of it, upon the two sides thereof, to be places for the staves to bear it withal.

28 And he made the staves of shittim wood, and overlaid them with gold.

Numbers 16

36 And the LORD spake unto Moses, saying,

37 Speak unto Eleazar the son of Aaron the priest, that he take up the censers out of the burning, and scatter thou the fire yonder; for they are hallowed.

38 The censers of these sinners against their own souls, let them make them broad plates for a covering of the altar: for they offered them before the LORD, therefore they are hallowed: and they shall be a sign unto the children of Israel.

39 And Eleazar the priest took the brasen censers, wherewith they that were burnt had offered; and they were made broad plates for a covering of the altar:

40 To be a memorial unto the children of Israel, that no stranger, which is not of the seed of Aaron, come near to offer incense before the LORD; that he be not as Korah, and as his company: as the LORD said to him by the hand of Moses.

N. Lavar of Brass for Washing the Priests Hands and Feet

Exodus 30

17 And the LORD spake unto Moses, saying,

18 Thou shalt also make a laver of brass, and his foot also of brass, to wash withal: and thou shalt put it between the tabernacle of the congregation and the altar, and thou shalt put water therein.

19 For Aaron and his sons shall wash their hands and their feet thereat:

20 When they go into the tabernacle of the congregation, they shall wash with water, that they die not; or when they come near to the altar to minister, to burn offering made by fire unto the LORD:

21 So they shall wash their hands and their feet, that they die not: and it shall be a statute for ever to them, even to him and to his seed throughout their generations.

Exodus 38
7 And he made the laver of brass, and the foot of it of brass, of the looking glasses of the women assembling, which assembled at the door of the tabernacle of the congregation.

O. Oil of Holy Ointment

Exodus 30
22 Moreover the LORD spake unto Moses, saying,
23 Take thou also unto thee principal spices, of pure myrrh five hundred shekels, and of sweet cinnamon half so much, even two hundred and fifty shekels, and of sweet calamus two hundred and fifty shekels,
24 And of cassia five hundred shekels, after the shekel of the sanctuary, and of oil olive an hin:
25 And thou shalt make it an oil of holy ointment, an ointment compound after the art of the apothecary: it shall be an holy anointing oil.

26 And thou shalt anoint the tabernacle of the congregation therewith, and the ark of the testimony,

And the table and all his vessels, and the candlestick and his vessels, and the altar of incense,

28 And the altar of burnt offering with all his vessels, and the laver and his foot.

29 And thou shalt sanctify them, that they may be most holy: whatsoever toucheth them shall be holy.

30 And thou shalt anoint Aaron and his sons, and consecrate them, that they may minister unto me in the priest's office.

31 And thou shalt speak unto the children of Israel, saying, This shall be an holy anointing oil unto me throughout your generations.

32 Upon man's flesh shall it not be poured, neither shall ye make any other like it, after the composition of it: it is holy, and it shall be holy unto you.

33 Whosoever compoundeth any like it, or whosoever putteth any of it upon a stranger, shall even be cut off from his people.

P. Holy Perfume

Exodus 30

34 And the LORD said unto Moses, Take unto thee sweet spices, stacte, and onycha, and galbanum; these sweet spices with pure frankincense: of each shall there be a like weight:

35 And thou shalt make it a perfume, a confection after the art of the apothecary, tempered together, pure and holy:

36 And thou shalt beat some of it very small, and put of it before the testimony in the tabernacle of the congregation, where I will meet with thee: it shall be unto you most holy.

37 And as for the perfume which thou shalt make, ye shall not make to yourselves according to the composition thereof: it shall be unto thee holy for the LORD.

38 Whosoever shall make like unto that, to smell thereto, shall even be cut off from his people.

Q. Aaron Given the Heave Offerings

Numbers 18

8 And the LORD spake unto Aaron, Behold, I also have given thee the charge of mine heave offerings of all the hallowed things of the children of Israel; unto thee have I given them by reason of the anointing, and to thy sons, by an ordinance for ever.

9   This shall be thine of the most holy things, reserved from the fire: every oblation of theirs, every meat offering of theirs, and every sin offering of theirs, and every trespass offering of theirs, which they shall render unto me, shall be most holy for thee and for thy sons.

10   In the most holy place shalt thou eat it; every male shall eat it: it shall be holy unto thee.

11   And this is thine; the heave offering of their gift, with all the wave offerings of the children of Israel: I have given them unto thee, and to thy sons and to thy daughters with thee, by a statute for ever: every one that is clean in thy house shall eat of it.

12   All the best of the oil, and all the best of the wine, and of the wheat, the firstfruits of them which they shall offer unto the LORD, them have I given thee.

13   And whatsoever is first ripe in the land, which they shall bring unto the LORD, shall be thine; every one that is clean in thine house shall eat of it.

14   Every thing devoted in Israel shall be thine.

15   Every thing that openeth the matrix in all flesh, which they bring unto the LORD, whether it be of men or beasts, shall be thine: nevertheless the firstborn of man shalt thou

surely redeem, and the firstling of unclean beasts shalt thou redeem.

16 And those that are to be redeemed from a month old shalt thou redeem, according to thine estimation, for the money of five shekels, after the shekel of the sanctuary, which is twenty gerahs.

17 But the firstling of a cow, or the firstling of a sheep, or the firstling of a goat, thou shalt not redeem; they are holy: thou shalt sprinkle their blood upon the altar, and shalt burn their fat for an offering made by fire, for a sweet savour unto the LORD.

18 And the flesh of them shall be thine, as the wave breast and as the right shoulder are thine.

19 All the heave offerings of the holy things, which the children of Israel offer unto the LORD, have I given thee, and thy sons and thy daughters with thee, by a statute for ever: it is a covenant of salt for ever before the LORD unto thee and to thy seed with thee.

The Hebrew Israelite Law Book

The Hebrew Israelite Law Book

TITLE 18 – OFFERINGS AND SACRIFICES

Chapter 1 – Sacrifice Preparation

Exodus 23
18 Thou shalt not offer the blood of my sacrifice with leavened bread; neither shall the fat of my sacrifice remain until the morning.

Exodus 34
25 Thou shalt not offer the blood of my sacrifice with leaven; neither shall the sacrifice of the feast of the passover be left unto the morning.

Leviticus 1
1   And the LORD called unto Moses, and spake unto him out of the tabernacle of the congregation, saying,
2   Speak unto the children of Israel, and say unto them, If any man of you bring an offering unto the LORD, ye shall bring your offering of the cattle, even of the herd, and of the flock.

Leviticus 2

13 And every oblation of thy meat offering shalt thou season with salt; neither shalt thou suffer the salt of the covenant of thy God to be lacking from thy meat offering: **with all thine offerings thou shalt offer salt.**

Leviticus 17

1 And the Lord spake unto Moses, saying,

2 Speak unto Aaron, and unto his sons, and unto all the children of Israel, and say unto them; This is the thing which the LORD hath commanded, saying,

3 What man soever there be of the house of Israel, that killeth an ox, or lamb, or goat, in the camp, or that killeth it out of the camp,

4 And bringeth it not unto the door of the tabernacle of the congregation, to offer an offering unto the LORD before the tabernacle of the LORD; blood shall be imputed unto that man; he hath shed blood; and that man shall be cut off from among his people:

5 To the end that the children of Israel may bring their sacrifices, which they offer in the open field, even that they may bring them unto the LORD, unto the door of the tabernacle of the congregation, unto the priest, and offer them for peace offerings unto the LORD.

6   And the priest shall sprinkle the blood upon the altar of the LORD at the door of the tabernacle of the congregation, and burn the fat for a sweet savour unto the LORD.

7   And they shall no more offer their sacrifices unto devils, after whom they have gone a whoring. This shall be a statute for ever unto them throughout their generations.

8   And thou shalt say unto them, Whatsoever man there be of the house of Israel, or of the strangers which sojourn among you, that offereth a burnt offering or sacrifice,

9   And bringeth it not unto the door of the tabernacle of the congregation, to offer it unto the LORD; even that man shall be cut off from among his people.

10 And whatsoever man there be of the house of Israel, or of the strangers that sojourn among you, that eateth any manner of blood; I will even set my face against that soul that eateth blood, and will cut him off from among his people.

11   For the life of the flesh is in the blood: and I have given it to you upon the altar to make an atonement for your souls: for it is the blood that maketh an atonement for the soul.

12 Therefore I said unto the children of Israel, No soul of you shall eat blood, neither

shall any stranger that sojourneth among you eat blood.

13 And whatsoever man there be of the children of Israel, or of the strangers that sojourn among you, which hunteth and catcheth any beast or fowl that may be eaten; he shall even pour out the blood thereof, and cover it with dust.

14 For it is the life of all flesh; the blood of it is for the life thereof: therefore I said unto the children of Israel, Ye shall eat the blood of no manner of flesh: for the life of all flesh is the blood thereof: whosoever eateth it shall be cut off.

15 And every soul that eateth that which died of itself, or that which was torn with beasts, whether it be one of your own country, or a stranger, he shall both wash his clothes, and bathe himself in water, and be unclean until the even: then shall he be clean.

16 But if he wash them not, nor bathe his flesh; then he shall bear his iniquity.

Leviticus 22

24 Ye shall not offer unto the LORD that which is bruised, or crushed, or broken, or cut; neither shall ye make any offering thereof in your land.

25 Neither from a stranger's hand shall ye offer the bread of your God of any of these;

because their corruption is in them, and blemishes be in them: they shall not be accepted for you.

26 And the LORD spake unto Moses, saying,

27 When a bullock, or a sheep, or a goat, is brought forth, then it shall be seven days under the dam; and from the eighth day and thenceforth it shall be accepted for an offering made by fire unto the LORD.

28 And whether it be cow or ewe, ye shall not kill it and her young both in one day.

Deuteronomy 17

1 Thou shalt not sacrifice unto the Lord thy God any bullock, or sheep, wherein is blemish, or any evil favouredness: for that is an abomination

unto the Lord thy God.

Chapter 2 - First Fruits

Exodus 22

29 Thou shalt not delay to offer the first of thy ripe fruits, and of thy liquors: the firstborn of thy sons shalt thou give unto me.

30 Likewise shalt thou do with thine oxen, and with thy sheep: seven days it shall be with his dam; on the eighth day thou shalt give it me.

Exodus 23

19 The first of the firstfruits of thy land thou shalt bring into the house of the LORD thy God. Thou shalt not seethe a kid in his mother's milk.

Exodus 34

26 The first of the firstfruits of thy land thou shalt bring unto the house of the LORD thy God. Thou shalt not seethe a kid in his mother's milk.

A. Meat Offering

a. Fine Flour

Leviticus 2

12   As for the oblation of the firstfruits, ye shall offer them unto the LORD: but they shall not be burnt on the altar for a sweet savour.

b. Corn

Leviticus 2

14   And if thou offer a meat offering of thy firstfruits unto the Lord, thou shalt offer for the meat offering of thy firstfruits green ears of corn dried by the fire, even corn beaten out of full ears.

15   And thou shalt put oil upon it, and lay frankincense thereon: it is a meat offering.

16   And the priest shall burn the memorial of it, part of the beaten corn thereof, and part of the oil thereof, with all the frankincense thereof: it is an offering made by fire unto the Lord.

Chapter 3 – Offering of Burnt Sacrifice

A. Herd

Leviticus 1

3   If his offering be a burnt sacrifice of the herd, let him offer a male without blemish: he shall offer it of his own voluntary will at the door of the tabernacle of the congregation before the LORD.

4   And he shall put his hand upon the head of the burnt offering; and it shall be accepted for him to make atonement for him.

5   And he shall kill the bullock before the LORD : and the priests, Aaron's sons, shall bring the blood, and sprinkle the blood round about upon the altar that is by the door of the tabernacle of the congregation.

6   And he shall flay the burnt offering, and cut it into his pieces.

7   And the sons of Aaron the priest shall put fire upon the altar, and lay the wood in order upon the fire:

8   And the priests, Aaron's sons, shall lay the parts, the head, and the fat, in order upon the wood that is on the fire which is upon the altar:

9   But his inwards and his legs shall he wash in water: and the priest shall burn all on the altar, to be a burnt sacrifice, an offering made by fire, of a sweet savour unto the LORD.

B. Flock

Leviticus 1

10   And if his offering be of the flocks, namely, of the sheep, or of the goats, for a burnt sacrifice; he shall bring it a male without blemish.

11   And he shall kill it on the side of the altar northward before the LORD : and the priests, Aaron's sons, shall sprinkle his blood round about upon the altar.

12   And he shall cut it into his pieces, with his head and his fat: and the priest shall lay them in order on the wood that is on the fire which is upon the altar:

13   But he shall wash the inwards and the legs with water: and the priest shall bring it all, and burn it upon the altar: it is a burnt sacrifice, an offering made by fire, of a sweet savour unto the Lord.

C. Fowls

Leviticus 1

14 And if the burnt sacrifice for his offering to the Lord be of fowls, then he shall bring his offering of turtledoves, or of young pigeons.

15 And the priest shall bring it unto the altar, and wring off his head, and burn it on the altar; and the blood thereof shall be wrung out at the side of the altar:

16 And he shall pluck away his crop with his feathers, and cast it beside the altar on the east part, by the place of the ashes:

17 And he shall cleave it with the wings thereof, but shall not divide it asunder: and the priest shall burn it upon the altar, upon the wood that is upon the fire: it is a burnt sacrifice, an offering made by fire, of a sweet savour unto the Lord.

Chapter 4 – Meat Offering (Baking)

A. Unbaked

Leviticus 2

1   And when any will offer a meat offering unto the Lord, his offering shall be of fine flour; and he shall pour oil upon it, and put frankincense thereon:

2   And he shall bring it to Aaron's sons the priests: and he shall take thereout his handful of the flour thereof, and of the oil thereof, with all the frankincense thereof; and the priest shall burn the memorial of it upon the altar, to be an offering made by fire, of a sweet savour unto the Lord:

3   And the remnant of the meat offering shall be Aaron's and his sons': it is a thing most holy of the offerings of the LORD made by fire.

B. Baked in an Oven

Leviticus 2

4   And if thou bring an oblation of a meat offering baken in the oven, it shall be unleavened cakes of fine flour mingled with oil, or unleavened wafers anointed with oil.

C. Baked in a Pan

Leviticus 2

5   And if thy oblation be a meat offering baken in a pan, it shall be of fine flour unleavened, mingled with oil.

6   Thou shalt part it in pieces, and pour oil thereon: it is a meat offering.

D. Baked in a Fryingpan

Leviticus 2

7   And if thy oblation be a meat offering baken in the fryingpan, it shall be made of fine flour with oil.

E. Priest Presentation

Leviticus 2

8   And thou shalt bring the meat offering that is made of these things unto the LORD: and when it is presented unto the priest, he shall bring it unto the altar.

9 And the priest shall take from the meat offering a memorial thereof, and shall burn it upon the altar: it is an offering made by fire, of a sweet savour unto the Lord.

10 And that which is left of the meat offering shall be Aaron's and his sons': it is a thing most holy of the offerings of the Lord made by fire.

11 No meat offering, which ye shall bring unto the LORD, shall be made with leaven: for ye shall burn no leaven, nor any honey, in any offering of the Lord made by fire.

Leviticus 2

13 And every oblation of thy meat offering shalt thou season with salt; neither shalt thou suffer the salt of the covenant of thy God to be lacking from thy meat offering: with all thine offerings thou shalt offer salt.

Chapter 5 – Sacrifice of Peace Offering

A. Herd

Leviticus 3

1   And if his oblation be a sacrifice of peace offering, if he offer it of the herd; whether it be a male or female, he shall offer it without blemish before the Lord.

2   And he shall lay his hand upon the head of his offering, and kill it at the door of the tabernacle of the congregation: and Aaron's sons the priests shall sprinkle the blood upon the altar round about.

3   And he shall offer of the sacrifice of the peace offering an offering made by fire unto the Lord; the fat that covereth the inwards, and all the fat that is upon the inwards,

4   And the two kidneys, and the fat that is on them, which is by the flanks, and the caul above the liver, with the kidneys, it shall he take away.

5   And Aaron's sons shall burn it on the altar upon the burnt sacrifice, which is upon

the wood that is on the fire: it is an offering made by fire, of a sweet savour unto the LORD.

B. Flock

a. Lamb

Leviticus 3

6   And if his offering for a sacrifice of peace offering unto the Lord be of the flock; male or female, he shall offer it without blemish.

7   If he offer a lamb for his offering, then shall he offer it before   the LORD.

8   And he shall lay his hand upon the head of his offering, and kill it before the tabernacle of the congregation: and Aaron's sons shall sprinkle the blood thereof round about upon the altar.

9   And he shall offer of the sacrifice of the peace offering an offering made by fire unto the Lord; the fat thereof, and the whole rump, it shall he take off hard by the backbone; and the fat that covereth the inwards, and all the fat that is upon the inwards,

10   And the two kidneys, and the fat that is upon them, which is by the flanks, and the caul above the liver, with the kidneys, it shall he take away.

11　And the priest shall burn it upon the altar: it is the food of the offering made by fire unto the Lord.

b. Goat

Leviticus 3

12　And if his offering be a goat, then he shall offer it before the Lord.

13　And he shall lay his hand upon the head of it, and kill it before the tabernacle of the congregation: and the sons of Aaron shall sprinkle the blood thereof upon the altar round about.

14　And he shall offer thereof his offering, even an offering made by fire unto the Lord; the fat that covereth the inwards, and all the fat that is upon the inwards,

15　And the two kidneys, and the fat that is upon them, which is by the flanks, and the caul above the liver, with the kidneys, it shall he take away.

16　And the priest shall burn them upon the altar: it is the food of the offering made by fire for a sweet savour: all the fat is the LORD'S.

17　It shall be a perpetual statute for your generations throughout all your dwellings, that ye eat neither fat nor blood.

The Hebrew Israelite Law Book

Chapter 6 – Sin Offering

A. If a Soul Sin Through Ignorance against any of the Commandments, If the Priest that is Anointed do Sin According to the Sin of the People

Leviticus 4

1   And the LORD spake unto Moses, saying,

2   Speak unto the Children of Israel, saying, If a soul shall sin through ignorance against any of the commandments of the LORD concerning things which ought not to be done, and shall do against any of them:

3   If the priest that is anointed do sin according to the sin of the people; then let him bring for his sin, which he hath sinned, a young bullock without blemish unto the LORD for a sin offering.

4   And he shall bring the bullock unto the door of the tabernacle of the congregation before the LORD ; and shall lay his hand upon the bullock's head, and kill the bullock before the LORD.

5   And the priest that is anointed shall take of the bullock's blood, and bring it to the tabernacle of the congregation:

6   And the priest shall dip his finger in the blood, and sprinkle of the blood seven times before the LORD, before the vail of the sanctuary.

7   And the priest shall put some of the blood upon the horns of the altar of sweet incense before the LORD, which is in the tabernacle of the congregation; and shall pour all the blood of the bullock at the bottom of the altar of the burnt offering, which is at the door of the tabernacle of the congregation.

8   And he shall take off from it all the fat of the bullock for the sin offering; the fat that covereth the inwards, and all the fat that is upon the inwards,

9   And the two kidneys, and the fat that is upon them, which is by the flanks, and the caul above the liver, with the kidneys, it shall he take away,

10 As it was taken off from the bullock of the sacrifice of peace offerings: and the priest shall burn them upon the altar of the burnt offering.

11 And the skin of the bullock, and all his flesh, with his head, and with his legs, and his inwards, and his dung,

12   Even the whole bullock shall he carry forth without the camp unto a clean place, where the ashes are poured out, and burn him on the wood with fire: where the ashes are poured out shall he be burnt.

B. If the whole congregation of Israel sin through ignorance, and the thing is hid from the eyes of the assembly, and they have done somewhat against any of the commandments of the LORD concerning things which should be done and are guilty

Leviticus 4

13   And if the whole congregation of Israel sin through ignorance, and the thing be hid from the eyes of the assembly, and they have done somewhat against any of the commandments of the LORD concerning things which should not be done, and are guilty;

14   When the sin, which they have sinned against it, is known, then the congregation shall offer a young bullock for the sin, and bring him before the tabernacle of the congregation.

15   And the elders of the congregation shall lay their hands upon the head of the

bullock before the LORD: and the bullock shall be killed before the LORD.

16 And the priest that is anointed shall bring of the bullock's blood to the tabernacle of the congregation:

17 And the priest shall dip his finger in some of the blood, and sprinkle it seven times before the Lord, even before the vail.

18 And he shall put some of the blood upon the horns of the altar which is before the Lord, that is in the tabernacle of the congregation, and shall pour out all the blood at the bottom of the altar of the burnt offering, which is at the door of the tabernacle of the congregation.

19 And he shall take all his fat from him, and burn it upon the altar.

20 And he shall do with the bullock as he did with the bullock for a sin offering, so shall he do with this: and the priest shall make an atonement for them, and it shall be forgiven them.

21 And he shall carry forth the bullock without the camp, and burn him as he burned the first bullock: it is a sin offering for the congregation.

C. A Ruler has Sinned and done somewhat through Ignorance any of the Commandments of the LORD his God concerning things which should not be done, and is guilty, Or if his sin, wherein he hath sinned, come to his knowledge

Leviticus 4

22 When a ruler hath sinned, and done somewhat through ignorance against any of the commandments of the Lord his God concerning things which should not be done, and is guilty;

23 Or if his sin, wherein he hath sinned, come to his knowledge; he shall bring his offering, a kid of the goats, a male without blemish:

24 And he shall lay his hand upon the head of the goat, and kill it in the place where they kill the burnt offering before the Lord: it is a sin offering.

25 And the priest shall take of the blood of the sin offering with his finger, and put it upon the horns of the altar of burnt offering, and shall pour out his blood at the bottom of the altar of burnt offering.

26 And he shall burn all his fat upon the altar, as the fat of the sacrifice of peace

offerings: and the priest shall make an atonement for him as concerning his sin, and it shall be forgiven him.

D. If any one of the Common People Sin through Ignorance, while he doeth somewhat against any of the Commandments of the LORD concerning things which ought not to be done, and be Guilty

a. Kid of the Goats

Leviticus 4

27 And if any one of the common people sin through ignorance, while he doeth somewhat against any of the commandments of the Lord concerning things which ought not to be done, and be guilty;

28 Or if his sin, which he hath sinned, come to his knowledge: then he shall bring his offering, a kid of the goats, a female without blemish, for his sin which he hath sinned.

29 And he shall lay his hand upon the head of the sin offering, and slay the sin offering in the place of the burnt offering.

30 And the priest shall take of the blood thereof with his finger, and put it upon the horns of the altar of burnt offering, and shall

pour out all the blood thereof at the bottom of the altar.

31 And he shall take away all the fat thereof, as the fat is taken away from off the sacrifice of peace offerings; and the priest shall burn it upon the altar for a sweet savour unto the Lord; and the priest shall make an atonement for him, and it shall be forgiven him.

b. Female Lamb

Leviticus 4

32 And if he bring a lamb for a sin offering, he shall bring it a female without blemish.

33 And he shall lay his hand upon the head of the sin offering, and slay it for a sin offering in the place where they kill the burnt offering.

34 And the priest shall take of the blood of the sin offering with his finger, and put it upon the horns of the altar of burnt offering, and shall pour out all the blood thereof at the bottom of the altar:

35 And he shall take away all the fat thereof, as the fat of the lamb is taken away from the sacrifice of the peace offerings; and the priest shall burn them upon the altar, according to the offerings made by fire unto the LORD: and the priest shall make an

atonement for his sin that he hath committed, and it shall be forgiven him.

Chapter 7 - Trespass Offering

A. Trespass Offering 1

Leviticus 5

1   And if a soul sin, and hear the voice of swearing, and is a witness, whether he hath seen or known of it; if he do not utter it, then he shall bear his iniquity.

2   Or if a soul touch any unclean thing, whether it be a carcase of an unclean beast, or a carcase of unclean cattle, or the carcase of unclean creeping things, and if it be hidden from him; he also shall be unclean, and guilty.

3   Or if he touch the uncleanness of man, whatsoever uncleanness it be that a man shall be defiled withal, and it be hid from him; when he knoweth of it, then he shall be guilty.

4   Or if a soul swear, pronouncing with his lips to do evil, or to do good, whatsoever it be that a man shall pronounce with an oath, and it be hid from him; when he knoweth of it, then he shall be guilty in one of these.

5   And it shall be, when he shall be guilty in one of these things, that he shall confess that he hath sinned in that thing:

a. Sin Offering

Leviticus 5
6   And he shall bring his trespass offering unto the LORD for his sin which he hath sinned, a female from the flock, a lamb or a kid of the goats, for a sin offering; and the priest shall make an atonement for him concerning his sin.

b. Sin and Burnt Offering

Leviticus 5
7   And if he be not able to bring a lamb, then he shall bring for his trespass, which he hath committed, two turtledoves, or two young pigeons, unto the LORD; one for a sin offering, and the other for a burnt offering.
8   And he shall bring them unto the priest, who shall offer that which is for the sin offering first, and wring off his head from his neck, but shall not divide it asunder:
9   And he shall sprinkle of the blood of the sin offering upon the side of the altar; and the rest of the blood shall be wrung out at the bottom of the altar: it is a sin offering.

10 And he shall offer the second for a burnt offering, according to the manner: and the priest shall make an atonement for him for his sin which he hath sinned, and it shall be forgiven him.

c. Sin and Meat Offering

Leviticus 5

11 But if he be not able to bring two turtledoves, or two young pigeons, then he that sinned shall bring for his offering the tenth part of an ephod of fine flour for a sin offering; he shall put no oil upon it, neither shall he put any frankincense thereon: for it is a sin offering.

12 Then shall he bring it to the priest, and the priest shall take his handful of it, even a memorial thereof, and burn it on the altar, according to the offerings made by fire unto the LORD : it is a sin offering.

13 And the priest shall make an atonement for him as touching his sin that he hath sinned in one of these, and it shall be forgiven him: and the remnant shall be the priest's, as a meat offering.

B. Trespass Offering 2

Leviticus 15

14 And the LORD spake unto
Moses, saying,

15 If a soul commit a trespass, and sin through ignorance, in the holy things of the LORD ; then he shall bring for his trespass unto the LORD a ram without blemish out of the flocks, with thy estimation by shekels of silver, after the shekels of the sanctuary, for a trespass offering:

16 And he shall make amends for the harm that he hath done in the holy thing, and shall add the fifth part thereto, and give it unto the priest: and the priest shall make an atonement for him with the ram of the trespass offering, and it shall be forgiven him.

C. Trespass Offering 3

Leviticus 5

17 And if a soul sin, and commit any of these things which are forbidden to be done by the commandments of the Lord; though he wist it not, yet is he guilty, and shall bear his iniquity.

18 And he shall bring a ram without blemish out of the flock, with thy estimation, for a trespass offering, unto the priest: and the priest shall make an atonement for him concerning his ignorance wherein he erred and wist it not, and it shall be forgiven him.

19 It is a trespass offering: he hath certainly trespassed against the LORD.

D. Trespass Offering 4

Leviticus 6

1   And the LORD spake unto Moses, saying,

2   If a soul sin, and commit a trespass against the LORD, and lie unto his neighbour in that which was delivered him to keep, or in fellowship, or in a thing taken away by violence, or hath deceived his neighbour;

3   Or have found that which was lost, and lieth concerning it, and sweareth falsely; in any of all these that a man doeth, sinning therein:

4   Then it shall be, because he hath sinned, and is guilty, that he shall restore that which he took violently away, or the thing which he hath deceitfully gotten, or that which was delivered him to keep, or the lost thing which he found,

5   Or all that about which he hath sworn falsely; he shall even restore it in the principal, and shall add the fifth part more thereto, and give it unto him to whom it appertaineth, in the day of his trespass offering.

6   And he shall bring his trespass offering unto the LORD, a ram without blemish out of the flock, with thy estimation, for a trespass offering, unto the priest:

7   And the priest shall make an atonement for him before the LORD : and it shall be forgiven him for any thing of all that he hath done in trespassing therein.

Chapter 8 – Law of the Burnt Offering

Leviticus 6

8   And the LORD spake unto Moses, saying,

9   Command Aaron and his sons, saying, This is the law of the burnt offering: It is the burnt offering, because of the burning upon the altar all night unto the morning, and the fire of the altar shall be burning in it.

10   And the priest shall put on his linen garment, and his linen breeches shall he put upon his flesh, and take up the ashes which the fire hath consumed with the burnt offering on the altar, and he shall put them beside the altar.

11   And he shall put off his garments, and put on other garments, and carry forth the ashes without the camp unto a clean place.

12   And the fire upon the altar shall be burning in it; it shall not be put out: and the priest shall burn wood on it every morning, and lay the burnt offering in order upon it;

and he shall burn thereon the fat of the peace offerings.

13   The fire shall ever be burning upon the altar; it shall never go out.

Leviticus 7

8   And the priest that offereth any man's burnt offering, even the priest shall have to himself the skin of the burnt offering which he hath offered.

Leviticus 22

17   And the LORD spake unto Moses, saying,

18   Speak unto Aaron, and to his sons, and unto all the children of Israel, and say unto them, Whatsoever he be of the house of Israel, or of the strangers in Israel, that will offer his oblation for all his vows, and for all his freewill offerings, which they will offer unto the LORD for a burnt offering;

19   Ye shall offer at your own will a male without blemish, of the beeves, of the sheep, or of the goats.

20   But whatsoever hath a blemish, that shall ye not offer: for it shall not be acceptable for you.

Chapter 9 – Law of the Meat Offering

Leviticus 6

14   And this is the law of the meat offering: the sons of Aaron shall offer it before the LORD, before the altar.

15   And he shall take of it his handful, of the flour of the meat offering, and of the oil thereof, and all the frankincense which is upon the meat offering, and shall burn it upon the altar for a sweet savour, even the memorial of it, unto the LORD.

16   And the remainder thereof shall Aaron and his sons eat: with unleavened bread shall it be eaten in the holy place; in the court of the tabernacle of the congregation they shall eat it.

17   It shall not be baken with leaven. I have given it unto them for their portion of my offerings made by fire; it is most holy, as is the sin offering, and as the trespass offering.

18   All the males among the children of Aaron shall eat of it. It shall be a statute for ever in your generations concerning the

offerings of the LORD made by fire: every one that toucheth them shall be holy.

Leviticus 7

9   And all the meat offering that is baken in the oven, and all that is dressed in the frying- pan, and in the pan, shall be the priest's that offereth it.

10   And every meat offering, mingled with oil, and dry, shall all the sons of Aaron have, one as much as another.

Leviticus 10

12   And Moses spake unto Aaron, and unto Eleazar and unto Ithamar, his sons that were left, Take the meat offering that remaineth of the offerings of the LORD made by fire, and eat it without leaven beside the altar: for it is most holy:

13   And ye shall eat it in the holy place, because it is thy due, and thy sons' due, of the sacrifices of the LORD made by fire: for so I am commanded.

Chapter 10 - Offering when Aaron and his Sons are Anointed

Leviticus 6

19 And the LORD spake unto Moses, saying,

20 This is the offering of Aaron and of his sons, which they shall offer unto the LORD in the day when he is anointed; the tenth part of an ephod of fine flour for a meat offering perpetual, half of it in the morning, and half thereof at night.

21 In a pan it shall be made with oil; and when it is baken, thou shalt bring it in: and the baken pieces of the meat offering shalt thou offer for a sweet savour unto the LORD.

22 And the priest of his sons that is anointed in his stead shall offer it: it is a statute for ever unto the LORD; it shall be wholly burnt.

23 For every meat offering for the priest shall be wholly burnt: it shall not be eaten.

The Hebrew Israelite Law Book

Chapter 11 – Law of the Sin Offering

Leviticus 6

24 And the LORD spake unto Moses, saying,

25 Speak unto Aaron and to his sons, saying, This is the law of the sin offering: In the place where the burnt offering is killed shall the sin offering be killed before the LORD: it is most holy.

26 The priest that offereth it for sin shall eat it: in the holy place shall it be eaten, in the court of the tabernacle of the congregation.

27 Whatsoever shall touch the flesh thereof shall be holy: and when there is sprinkled of the blood thereof upon any garment, thou shalt wash that whereon it was sprinkled in the holy place.

28 But the earthen vessel wherein it is sodden shall be broken: and if it be sodden in a brasen pot, it shall be both scoured, and rinsed in water.

29 All the males among the priests shall eat thereof: it is most holy.

30 And no sin offering, whereof any of the blood is brought into the tabernacle of the congregation to reconcile withal in the holy place, shall be eaten: it shall be burnt in the fire.

Chapter 12 – Law of the Trespass Offering

Leviticus 7

1   Like wise this is the law of the trespass offering: it is most holy.

2   In the place where they kill the burnt offering shall they kill the trespass offering: and the blood thereof shall he sprinkle round about upon the altar.

3   And he shall offer of it all the fat thereof; the rump, and the fat that covereth the inwards,

4   And the two kidneys, and the fat that is on them, which is by the flanks, and the caul that is above the liver, with the kidneys, it shall he take away:

5   And the priest shall burn them upon the altar for an offering made by fire unto the Lord : it is a trespass offering.

6   Every male among the priests shall eat thereof: it shall be eaten in the holy place: it is most holy.

7   As the sin offering is, so is the trespass offering: there is one law for them: the priest

that maketh atonement therewith shall have it.

Chapter 13 – Law of the Sacrifice of Peace Offerings

A. Thanksgiving Offering

Leviticus 7

11   And this is the law of the sacrifice of peace offerings, which he shall offer unto the Lord.

12   If he offer it for a thanksgiving, then he shall offer with the sacrifice of thanksgiving unleavened cakes mingled with oil, and unleavened wafers anointed with oil, and cakes mingled with oil, of fine flour, fried.

13   Besides the cakes, he shall offer for his offering leavened bread with the sacrifice of thanksgiving of his peace offerings.

14   And of it he shall offer one out of the whole oblation for an heave offering unto the LORD, and it shall be the priest's that sprinkleth the blood of the peace offerings.

15 And the flesh of the sacrifice of his peace offerings for thanksgiving shall be eaten the same day that it is offered; he shall not leave any of it until the morning.

Leviticus 22

29 And when ye will offer a sacrifice of thanksgiving unto the LORD, offer it at your own will.

30 On the same day it shall be eaten up; ye shall leave none of it until the morrow: I am the LORD.

31 Therefore shall ye keep my commandments, and do them; I am the LORD.

B. Vow or Voluntary Offering

16 But if the sacrifice of his offering be a vow, or a voluntary offering, it shall be eaten the same day that he offereth his sacrifice: and on the morrow also the remainder of it shall be eaten:

17 But the remainder of the flesh of the sacrifice on the third day shall be burnt with fire.

18 And if any of the flesh of the sacrifice of his peace offerings be eaten at all on the third day, it shall not be accepted, neither shall it be imputed unto him that offereth it: it shall be

an abomination, and the soul that eateth of it shall bear his iniquity.

19 And the flesh that toucheth any unclean thing shall not be eaten; it shall be burnt with fire: and as for the flesh, all that be clean shall eat thereof.

20 But the soul that eateth of the flesh of the sacrifice of peace offerings, that pertain unto the Lord, having his uncleanness upon him, even that soul shall be cut off from his people.

21 Moreover the soul that shall touch any unclean thing, as the uncleanness of man, or any unclean beast, or any abominable unclean thing, and eat of the flesh of the sacrifice of peace offerings, which pertain unto the Lord, even that soul shall be cut off from his people.

Leviticus 7

28 And the LORD spake unto Moses, saying,

29 Speak unto the children of Israel, saying, He that offereth the sacrifice of his peace offerings unto the LORD shall bring his oblation unto the LORD of the sacrifice of his peace offerings.

30 His own hands shall bring the offerings of the Lord made by fire, the fat with the

breast, it shall he bring, that the breast may be waved for a wave offering before the Lord.

31 And the priest shall burn the fat upon the altar: but the breast shall be Aaron's and his sons'.

32 And the right shoulder shall ye give unto the priest for an heave offering of the sacrifices of your peace offerings.

33 He among the sons of Aaron, that offereth the blood of the peace offerings, and the fat, shall have the right shoulder for his part.

34 For the wave breast and the heave shoulder have I taken of the children of Israel from off the sacrifices of their peace offerings, and have given them unto Aaron the priest and unto his sons by a statute for ever from among the children of Israel.

35 This is the portion of the anointing of Aaron, and of the anointing of his sons, out of the offerings of the Lord made by fire, in the day when he presented them to minister unto the Lord in the priest's office;

36 Which the Lord commanded to be given them of the children of Israel, in the day that he anointed them, by a statute for ever throughout their generations.

37 This is the law of the burnt offering, of the meat offering, and of the sin offering, and of the trespass offering, and of the

consecrations, and of the sacrifice of the peace offerings;

38 Which the LORD commanded Moses in mount Sinai, in the day that he commanded the children of Israel to offer their oblations unto the LORD, in the wilderness of Sinai.

Leviticus 10

14 And the wave breast and heave shoulder shall ye eat in a clean place; thou, and thy sons, and thy daughters with thee: for they be thy due, and thy sons' due, which are given out of the sacrifices of peace offerings of the children of Israel.

15 The heave shoulder and the wave breast shall they bring with the offerings made by fire of the fat, to wave it for a wave offering before the LORD; and it shall be thine, and thy sons' with thee, by a statute for ever; as the LORD hath commanded.

Leviticus 19

5 And if ye offer a sacrifice of peace offerings unto the LORD, ye shall offer it at your own will.

6 It shall be eaten the same day ye offer it, and on the morrow: and if ought remain until the third day, it shall be burnt in the fire.

7 And if it be eaten at all on the third day, it is abominable; it shall not be accepted.

8 Therefore every one that eateth it shall bear his iniquity, because he hath profaned the hallowed thing of the Lord: and that soul shall be cut off from among his people.

Leviticus 22

21 And whosoever offereth a sacrifice of peace offerings unto the LORD to accomplish his vow, or a freewill offering in beeves or sheep, it shall be perfect to be accepted; there shall be no blemish therein.

22 Blind, or broken, or maimed, or having a wen, or scurvy, or scabbed, ye shall not offer these unto the LORD, nor make an offering by fire of them upon the altar unto the LORD.

23 Either a bullock or a lamb that hath anything superfluous or lacking in his parts, that mayest thou offer for a freewill offering ; but for a vow it shall not be accepted.

Chapter 14 – When Israel first comes into the Land

A. Making Offerings

Numbers 15

1 And the LORD spake unto Moses, saying,

2 Speak unto the children of Israel, and say unto them, When ye be come into the land of your habitations, which I give unto you,

3 And will make an offering by fire unto the LORD, a burnt offering, or a sacrifice in performing a vow, or in a freewill offering, or in your solemn feasts, to make a sweet savour unto the LORD, of the herd, or of the flock:

Numbers 15

11 Thus shall it be done for one bullock, or for one ram, or for a lamb, or a kid.

12 According to the number that ye shall prepare, so shall ye do to every one according to their number.

13 All that are born of the country shall do these things after this manner, in offering an

offering made by fire, of a sweet savour unto the LORD.

14 And if a stranger sojourn with you, or whosoever be among you in your generations, and will offer an offering made by fire, of a sweet savour unto the LORD ; as ye do, so he shall do.

15 One ordinance shall be both for you of the congregation, and also for the stranger that sojourneth with you, an ordinance for ever in your generations: as ye are, so shall the stranger be before the LORD.

16 One law and one manner shall be for you, and for the stranger that sojourneth with you.

a. Flock

Meat Offering for One Lamb

Numbers 15

4 Then shall he that offereth his offering unto the LORD bring a meat offering of a tenth deal of flour mingled with the fourth part of an hin of oil.

5 And the fourth part of an hin of wine for a drink offering shalt thou prepare with the burnt offering or sacrifice, for one lamb.

Meat Offering for One Ram

Numbers 15

6   Or for a ram, thou shalt prepare for a meat offering two tenth deals of flour mingled with the third part of an hin of oil.

7   And for a drink offering thou shalt offer the third part of an hin or wine, for a sweet savour unto the LORD.

b. Herd

Meat Offering for One Bullock

Numbers 15

8   And when thou preparest a bullock for a burnt offering, or for a sacrifice in performing a vow, or peace offerings unto the LORD:

9   Then shall he bring with a bullock a meat offering of three tenth deals of flour mingled with half an hin of oil.

10 And thou shalt bring for a drink offering half an hin of wine, for an offering made by fire, of a sweet savour unto the LORD.

B. When Israel first Eats the Bread of the Land

Numbers 15

17 And the LORD spake unto Moses, saying,

18 Speak unto the children of Israel, and say unto them, When ye come into the land whither I bring you,

19 Then it shall be, that, when ye eat of the bread of the land, ye shall offer up an heave offering unto the LORD.

20 Ye shall offer up a cake of the first of your dough for an heave offering: as ye do the heave offering of the threshing floor, so shall ye heave it.

21 Of the first of your dough ye shall give unto the LORD an heave offering in your generations.

C. If the Children of Israel Erred and Don't Keep Commandments

Numbers 15

22 And if ye have erred, and not observed all these commandments, which the LORD hath spoken unto Moses,

23 Even all that the LORD hath commanded you by the hand of Moses, from the day that the LORD commanded Moses, and henceforward among your generations;

a. Sin through Ignorance Without the Knowledge of the Congregation

Numbers 15

24 Then it shall be, if ought be committed by ignorance without the knowledge of the congregation, that all the congregation shall offer one young bullock for a burnt offering, for a sweet savour unto the Lord, with his meat offering, and his drink offering, according to the manner, and one kid of the goats for a sin offering.

25 And the priest shall make an atonement for all the congregation of the children of Israel, and it shall be forgiven them; for it is ignorance: and they shall bring their offering, a sacrifice made by fire unto the LORD, and their sin offering before the LORD, for their ignorance:

26 And it shall be forgiven all the congregation of the children of Israel, and the stranger that sojourneth among them; seeing all the people were in ignorance.

b. Sin Through Ignorance

Numbers 15

27 And if any soul sin through ignorance, then he shall bring a she goat of the first year for a sin offering.

28 And the priest shall make an atonement for the soul that sinneth ignorantly, when he sinneth by ignorance before the LORD, to make an atonement for him; and it shall be forgiven him.

29 Ye shall have one law for him that sinneth through ignorance, both for him that is born among the children of Israel, and for the stranger that sojourneth among them.

c. Soul that Doeth Ought Presumptuously

Numbers 15

30 But the soul that doeth ought presumptuously, whether he be bora in the land, or a stranger, the same reproacheth the LORD ; and that soul shall be cut off from among his people.

31 Because he hath despised the word of the LORD, and hath broken his commandment, that soul shall utterly be cut off; his iniquity shall be upon him.

D. Location of Sacrifices

Deuteronomy 12

1 These are the statutes and judgments, which ye shall observe to do in the land, which the LORD God of thy fathers giveth

thee to possess it, all the days that ye live upon the earth.

2   Ye shall utterly destroy all the places, wherein the nations which ye shall possess served their gods, upon the high mountains, and upon the hills, and under every green tree:

3   And ye shall overthrow their altars, and break their pillars, and burn their groves with fire; and ye shall hew down the graven images of their gods, and destroy the names of them out of that place.

4   Ye shall not do so unto the LORD your God.

5   But unto the place which the LORD your God shall choose out of all your tribes to put his name there, even unto his habitation shall ye seek, and thither thou shalt come:

6   And thither ye shall bring your burnt offerings, and your sacrifices, and your tithes, and heave offerings of your hand, and your vows, and your freewill offerings, and the firstlings of your herds and of your flocks:

7   And there ye shall eat before the LORD your God, and ye shall rejoice in all that ye put your hand unto, ye and your households, wherein the LORD thy God hath blessed thee.

8   Ye shall not do after all the things that we do here this day, every man whatsoever is right in his own eyes.

9 For ye are not as yet come to the rest and to the inheritance, which the LORD your God giveth you.

10 But when ye go over Jordan, and dwell in the land which the LORD your God giveth you to inherit, and when he giveth you rest from all your enemies round about, so that ye dwell in safety;

11 Then there shall be a place which the LORD your God shall choose to cause his name to dwell there; thither shall ye bring all that I command you; your burnt offerings, and your sacrifices, your tithes, and the heave offering of your hand, and all your choice vows which ye vow unto the LORD:

12 And ye shall rejoice before the Lord your God, ye, and your sons, and your daughters, and your menservants, and your maidservants, and the Levite that is within your gates; forasmuch as he hath no part nor inheritance with you.

13 Take heed to thyself that thou offer not thy burnt offerings in every place that thou seest:

14 But in the place which the LORD shall choose in one of thy tribes, there thou shalt offer thy burnt offerings, and there thou shalt do all that I command thee.

15 Notwithstanding thou mayest kill and eat flesh in all thy gates, whatsoever thy soul

lusteth after, according to the blessing of the LORD thy God which he hath given thee: the unclean and the clean may eat thereof, as of the roebuck, and as of the hart.

16   Only ye shall not eat the blood; ye shall pour it upon the earth as water.

17   Thou mayest not eat within thy gates the tithe of thy corn, or of thy wine, or of thy oil, or the firstlings of thy herds or of thy flock, nor any of thy vows which thou vowest, nor thy freewill offerings, or heave offering of thine hand:

18   But thou must eat them before the LORD thy God in the place which the LORD thy God shall choose, thou, and thy son, and thy daughter, and thy manservant, and thy maidservant, and the Levite that is within thy gates: and thou shalt rejoice before the LORD thy God in all that thou puttest thine hands unto.

19   Take heed to thyself that thou forsake not the Levite as long as thou livest upon the earth.

20   When the LORD thy God shall enlarge thy border, as he hath promised thee, and thou shalt say, I will eat flesh, because thy soul longeth to eat flesh; thou mayest eat flesh, whatsoever thy soul lusteth after.

21   If the place which the LORD thy God hath chosen to put his name there be too far

from thee, then thou shalt kill of thy herd and of thy flock, which the LORD hath given thee, as I have commanded thee, and thou shalt eat in thy gates whatsoever thy soul lusteth after.

22 Even as the roebuck and the hart is eaten, so thou shalt eat them: the unclean and the clean shall eat of them alike.

23 Only be sure that thou eat not the blood: for the blood is the life; and thou mayest not eat the life with the flesh.

24 Thou shalt not eat it; thou shalt pour it upon the earth as water.

25 Thou shalt not eat it; that it may go well with thee, and with thy children after thee, when thou shalt do that which is right in the sight of the LORD.

26 Only thy holy things which thou hast, and thy vows, thou shalt take, and go unto the place which the LORD shall choose:

27 And thou shalt offer thy burnt offerings, the flesh and the blood, upon the altar of the LORD thy God: and the blood of thy sacrifices shall be poured out upon the altar of the LORD thy God, and thou shalt eat the flesh.

28 Observe and hear all these words which I command thee, that it may go well with thee, and with thy children after thee for ever, when thou doest that which is good and right in the sight of the LORD thy God.

E. First of All the Fruit of the Earth

Deuteronomy 26

1   And it shall be, when thou art come in unto the land which the Lord thy God giveth thee for an inheritance, and possessest it, and dwellest therein;

2   That thou shalt take of the first of all the fruit of the earth, which thou shalt bring of thy land that the LORD thy God giveth thee, and shalt put it in a basket, and shalt go unto the place which the LORD thy God shall choose to place his name there.

3   And thou shalt go unto the priest that shall be in those days, and say unto him, I profess this day unto the LORD thy God, that I am come unto the country which the LORD sware unto our fathers for to give us.

4   And the priest shall take the basket out of thine hand, and set it down before the altar of the LORD thy God.

5   And thou shalt speak and say before the LORD thy God, A Syrian ready to perish was my father, and he went down into Egypt, and sojourned there with a few, and became there a nation, great, mighty, and populous:

6   And the Egyptians evil entreated us, and afflicted us, and laid upon us hard bondage:

7   And when we cried unto the LORD God of our fathers, the LORD heard our voice, and looked on our affliction, and our labour, and our oppression:

8   And the LORD brought us forth out of Egypt with a mighty hand, and with an outstretched arm, and with great terribleness, and with signs, and with wonders:

9   And he hath brought us into this place, and hath given us this land, even a land that floweth with milk and honey.

10   And now, behold, I have brought the firstfruits of the land, which thou, O LORD, hast given me. And thou shalt set it before the LORD thy God, and worship before the LORD thy God:

11   And thou shalt rejoice in every good thing which the LORD thy God hath given unto thee, and unto thine house, thou, and the Levite, and the stranger that is among you.

Chapter 15 – Day by Day

Numbers 28

1   And the LORD spake unto Moses, saying,

2   Command the children of Israel, and say unto them, My offering, and my bread for my sacrifices made by fire, for a sweet savour unto me, shall ye observe to offer unto me in their due season.

3   And thou shalt say unto them, This is the offering made by fire which ye shall offer unto the LORD; two lambs of the first year without spot day by day, for a continual burnt offering.

4   The one lamb shalt thou offer in the morning, and the other lamb shalt thou offer at even;

5   And a tenth part of an ephah of flour for a meat offering, mingled with the fourth part of an hin of beaten oil.

6   It is a continual burnt offering, which was ordained in mount Sinai for a sweet savour, a sacrifice made by fire unto the LORD.

7   And the drink offering thereof shall be the fourth part of an hin for the one lamb: in the holy place shalt thou cause the strong wine to be poured unto the LORD for a drink offering.

8   And the other lamb shalt thou offer at even: as the meat offering of the morning, and as the drink offering thereof, thou shalt offer it, a sacrifice made by fire, of a sweet savour unto the LORD.

Chapter 16 – On the Sabbath Day

Numbers 28

9   And on the sabbath day two lambs of the first year without spot, and two tenth deals of flour for a meat offering, mingled with oil, and the drink offering thereof:

10   This is the burnt offering of every sabbath, beside the continual burnt offering, and his drink offering.

Chapter 17 – In the Beginning of Every Month

Numbers 28

11 And in the beginnings of your months ye shall offer a burnt offering unto the LORD; two young bullocks, and one ram, seven lambs of the first year without spot;

12 And three tenth deals of flour for a meat offering, mingled with oil, for one bullock; and two tenth deals of flour for a meat offering, mingled with oil, for one ram;

13 And a several tenth deal of flour mingled with oil for a meat offering unto one lamb; for a burnt offering of a sweet savour, a sacrifice made by fire unto the LORD.

14 And their drink offerings shall be half an hin of wine unto a bullock, and the third part of an hin unto a ram, and a fourth part of an hin unto a lamb: this is the burnt offering of every month throughout the months of the year.

15 And one kid of the goats for a sin offering unto the LORD shall be offered, beside the continual burnt offering, and his drink offering.

TITLE 19 – CLEAN AND UNCLEAN

Exodus 22

31 And ye shall be holy men unto me: neither shall ye eat any flesh that is torn of beasts in the field; ye shall cast it to the dogs.

Leviticus 3

It shall be a perpetual statute for your generations throughout all your dwellings, that ye eat neither fat nor blood.

Leviticus 7

22 And the LORD spake unto Moses, saying,

23 Speak unto the children of Israel, saying, Ye shall eat no manner of fat, of ox, or of sheep, or of goat.

24 And the fat of the beast that dieth of itself, and the fat of that which is torn with beasts, may be used in any other use: but ye shall in no wise eat of it.

25 For whosoever eateth the fat of the beast, of which men offer an offering made by

fire unto the Lord, even the soul that eateth it shall be cut off from his people.

26 Moreover ye shall eat no manner of blood, whether it he of fowl or of beast, in any of your dwellings.

27 Whatsoever soul it be that eateth any manner of blood, even that soul shall be cut off from his people.

Leviticus 11

45 For I am the LORD that bringeth you up out of the land of Egypt, to be your God: ye shall therefore be holy, for I am holy.

46 This is the law of the beasts, and of the fowl, and of every living creature that moveth in the waters, and of every creature that creepeth upon the earth:

47 To make a difference between the unclean and the clean, and between the beast that may be eaten and the beast that may not be eaten.

Leviticus 19

26 Ye shall not eat any thing with the blood: neither shall ye use enchantment, nor observe times.

Deuteronomy 14

21 Ye shall not eat of any thing that dieth of itself: thou shalt give it unto the stranger

that is in thy gates, that he may eat it; or thou mayest sell it unto an alien: for thou art an holy people unto the LORD thy God. Thou shalt not seethe a kid in his mother's milk.

Chapter 1-The Beast

Leviticus 11

1   And the LORD spake unto Moses and to Aaron, saying unto them,

2   Speak unto the children of Israel, saying, These are the beasts which ye shall eat among all the beasts that are on the earth.

3   Whatsoever parteth the hoof, and is clovenfooted, and cheweth the cud, among the beasts, that shall ye eat.

4   Nevertheless these shall ye not eat of them that chew the cud, or of them that divide the hoof: as the camel, because he cheweth the cud, but divideth not the hoof; he is unclean unto you.

5   And the coney, because he cheweth the cud, but divideth not the hoof; he is unclean unto you.

6   And the hare, because he cheweth the cud, but divideth not the hoof; he is unclean unto you.

7   And the swine, though he divide the hoof, and be cloven-footed, yet he cheweth not the cud; he is unclean to you.

8   Of their flesh shall ye not eat, and their carcase shall ye not touch; they are unclean to you.

Leviticus 11

26 The carcases of every beast which divideth the hoof, and is not clovenfooted, nor cheweth the cud, are unclean unto you: every one that toucheth them shall be unclean.

27 And whatsoever goeth upon his paws, among all manner of beasts that go on all four, those are unclean unto you: whoso toucheth their carcase shall be unclean until the even.

28 And he that beareth the carcase of them shall wash his clothes, and be unclean until the even: they are unclean unto you.

Leviticus 11

39 And if any beast, of which ye may eat, die; he that toucheth the carcase thereof shall be unclean until the even.

40 And he that eateth of the carcase of it shall wash his clothes, and be unclean until the even: he also that beareth the carcase of it shall wash his clothes, and be unclean until the even.

Deuteronomy 14

3   Thou shalt not eat any abominable thing.

4   These are the beasts which ye shall eat: the ox, the sheep, and the goat,

5   The hart, and the roebuck, and the fallow deer, and the wild goat, and the pygarg, and the wild ox, and the chamois.

6   And every beast that parteth the hoof, and cleaveth the cleft into two claws, and cheweth the cud among the beasts, that ye shall eat.

7   Nevertheless these ye shall not eat of them that chew the cud, or of them that divide the cloven hoof; as the camel, and the hare, and the coney: for they chew the cud, but divide not the hoof; therefore they are unclean unto you.

8   And the swine, because it divideth the hoof, yet cheweth not the cud, it is unclean unto you: ye shall not eat of their flesh, nor touch their dead carcase.

Chapter 2-In the Waters

Leviticus 11

9   These shall ye eat of all that are in the waters: whatsoever hath fins and scales in the waters, in the seas, and in the rivers, them shall ye eat.

10   And all that have not fins and scales in the seas, and in the rivers, of all that move in the waters, and of any living thing which is in the waters, they shall he an abomination unto you:

11   They shall be even an abomination unto you; ye shall not eat of their flesh, but ye shall have their carcases in abomination.

12   Whatsoever hath no fins nor scales in the waters, that shall be an abomination unto you.

Deuteronomy 14

9   These ye shall eat of all that are in the waters: all that have fins and scales shall ye eat:

10   And whatsoever hath not fins and scales ye may not eat; it is unclean unto you.

The Hebrew Israelite Law Book

Chapter 3-Fowls

Leviticus 11

13 And these are they which ye shall have in abomination among the fowls; they shall not be eaten, they are an abomination: the eagle, and the ossifrage, and the ospray,

14 And the vulture, and the kite after his kind;

15 Every raven after his kind;

16 And the owl, and the night hawk, and the cuckow, and the hawk after his kind,

17 And the little owl, and the cormorant, and the great owl,

18 And the swan, and the pelican, and the gier eagle,

19 And the stork, the heron after her kind, and the lapwing, and the bat.

Deuteronomy 14

11 Of all clean birds ye shall eat.

12 But these are they of which ye shall not eat: the eagle, and the ossifrage, and the ospray,

13 And the glede, and the kite, and the vulture after his kind,

14 And every raven after his kind,

15 And the owl, and the night hawk, and the cuckow, and the hawk after his kind,

16 The little owl, and the great owl, and the swan,

17 And the pelican, and the gier eagle, and the cormorant,

18 And the stork, and the heron after her kind, and the lapwing, and the bat

19And every creeping thing that flieth is unclean unto you: they shall not be eaten.

20But of all clean fowls ye may eat.

Chapter 4-Fowls that Creep

Leviticus 11

20 All fowls that creep, going upon all four, shall be an abomination unto you.

21 Yet these may ye eat of every flying creeping tiling that goeth upon all four, which have legs above their feet, to leap withal upon the earth;

22 Even these of them ye may eat; the locust after his kind, and the bald locust after his kind, and the beetle after his kind, and the grasshopper after his kind.

23 But all other flying creeping things, which have four feet, shall be an abomination unto you.

And for these ye shall be unclean: whosoever toucheth the carcase of them shall be unclean until the even.

25 And whosoever beareth ought of the carcase of them shall wash his clothes, and be unclean until the even.

Deuteronomy 14

19 And every creeping thing that flieth is unclean unto you: they shall not be eaten.

20 But all clean fowls ye may eat.

Chapter 5-The Creeping Things

Leviticus 11

29 These also shall be unclean unto you among the creeping things that creep upon the earth; the weasel, and the mouse, and the tortoise after his kind,

30 And the ferret, and the chameleon, and the lizard, and the snail, and the mole.

31 These are unclean to you among all that creep: whosoever doth touch them, when they be dead, shall be unclean until the even.

32 And upon whatsoever any of them, when they are dead, doth fall, it shall be unclean; whether it be any vessel of wood, or raiment, or skin, or sack, whatsoever vessel it be, wherein any work is done, it must be put into water, and it shall be unclean until the even; so it shall be cleansed.

33 And every earthen vessel, where into any of them falleth, whatsoever is in it shall be unclean; and ye shall break it.

34 Of all meat which may be eaten, that on which such water cometh shall be unclean:

and all drink that may be drunk in every such vessel shall be unclean.

35 And every thing whereupon any part of their carcase falleth shall be unclean; whether it be oven, or ranges for pots, they shall be broken down: for they are unclean, and shall be unclean unto you.

36 Nevertheless a fountain or pit, wherein there is plenty of water, shall be clean: but that which toucheth their carcase shall be unclean.

37 And if any part of their carcase fall upon any sowing seed which is to be sown, it shall be clean.

38 But if any water be put upon the seed, and any part of their carcase fall thereon, it shall be unclean unto you.

Leviticus 11

41 And every creeping thing that creepeth upon the earth shall be an abomination; it shall not be eaten.

42 Whatsoever goeth upon the belly, and whatsoever goeth upon all four, or whatsoever hath more feet among all creeping things that creep upon the earth, them ye shall not eat; for they are an abomination.

43 Ye shall not make your selves abominable with any creeping thing that

creepeth, neither shall ye make yourselves unclean with them, that ye should be defiled thereby.

44 For I am the LORD your God: ye shall therefore sanctify yourselves, and ye shall be holy; for I am holy: neither shall ye defile yourselves with any manner of creeping thing that creepeth upon the earth.

Chapter 6-Woman that has Conceived

A. A Man Child

Leviticus 12

1   And the LORD spake unto Moses, saying,

2   Speak unto the children of Israel, saying, If a woman have conceived seed, and born a man child: then she shall be unclean seven days; according to the days of the separation for her infirmity shall she be unclean.

3   And in the eighth day the flesh of his foreskin shall be circumcised.

4   And she shall then continue in the blood of her purifying three and thirty days; she shall touch no hallowed thing, nor come into the sanctuary, until the days of her purifying be fulfilled.

B. A Maid Child

Leviticus 12

5   But if she bear a maid child, then she shall be unclean two weeks, as in her separation: and she shall continue in the blood of her purifying threescore and six days.

C. Burnt Offering

Leviticus 12

6   And when the days of her purifying are fulfilled, for a son, or for a daughter, she shall bring a lamb of the first year for a burnt offering, and a young pigeon, or a turtledove, for a sin offering, unto the door of the tabernacle of the congregation, unto the priest:

7   Who shall offer it before the LORD, and make an atonement for her; and she shall be cleansed from the issue of her blood. This is the law for her that hath born a male or a female.

8   And if she be not able to bring a lamb, then she shall bring two turtles, or two young pigeons; the one for the burnt offering, and the other for a sin offering: and the priest shall make an atonement for her, and she shall be clean.

The Hebrew Israelite Law Book

Chapter 7-Leprosy

Deuteronomy 24

8   Take heed in the plague of leprosy, that thou observe diligently, and do according to all that the priests the Levites shall teach you: as I commanded them, so ye shall observe to do.

9   Remember what the LORD thy God did unto Miriam by the way, after that ye were come forth out of Egypt.

A. On the Skin

Leviticus 13

1   And the LORD spake unto Moses and Aaron, saying,

2   When a man shall have in the skin of his flesh a rising, a scab, or bright spot, and it be in the skin of his flesh like the plague of leprosy; then he shall be brought unto Aaron the priest, or unto one of his sons the priests:

3   And the priest shall look on the plague in the skin of the flesh: and when the hair in the plague is turned white, and the plague in

sight be deeper than the skin of his flesh, it is a plague of leprosy: and the priest shall look on him, and pronounce him unclean.

4   If the bright spot be white in the skin of his flesh, and in sight be not deeper than the skin, and the hair thereof be not turned white; then the priest shall shut up him that hath the plague seven days:

5   And the priest shall look on him the seventh day: and, behold, if the plague in his sight be at a stay, and the plague spread not in the skin; then the priest shall shut him up seven days more:

6   And the priest shall look on him again the seventh day: and, behold, if the plague be somewhat dark, and the plague spread not in the skin, the priest shall pronounce him clean: it is but a scab: and he shall wash his clothes, and be clean.

7   But if the scab spread much abroad in the skin, after that he hath been seen of the priest for his cleansing, he shall be seen of the priest again:

8   And if the priest see that, behold, the scab spreadeth in the skin, then the priest shall pronounce him unclean: it is a leprosy.

9   When the plague of leprosy is in a man, then he shall be brought unto the priest;

10 And the priest shall see him : and, behold, if the rising be white in the skin, and

it have turned the hair white, and there be quick raw flesh in the rising;

11   It is an old leprosy in the skin of his flesh, and the priest shall pronounce him unclean, and shall not shut him up: for he is unclean.

12   And if a leprosy break out abroad in the skin, and the leprosy cover all the skin of him that hath the plague from his head even to his foot, wheresoever the priest looketh;

13   Then the priest shall consider: and, behold, if the leprosy have covered all his flesh, he shall pronounce him clean that hath the plague: it is all turned white: he is clean.

14   But when raw flesh appeareth in him, he shall be unclean.

15   And the priest shall see the raw flesh, and pronounce him to be unclean: for the raw flesh is unclean: it is a leprosy.

16   Or if the raw flesh turn again, and be changed unto white, he shall come unto the priest;

17   And the priest shall see him: and, behold, if the plague be turned into white; then the priest shall pronounce him clean that hath the plague: he is clean.

18   The flesh also, in which, even in the skin thereof, was a boil, and is healed,

19   And in the place of the boil there be a white rising, or a bright spot, white, and

somewhat reddish, and it be shewed to the priest;

20 And if, when the priest seeth it, behold, it be in sight lower than the skin, and the hair thereof be turned white; the priest shall pronounce him unclean: it is a plague of leprosy broken out of the boil.

21 But if the priest look on it, and, behold, there be no white hairs therein, and if it be not lower than the skin, but be somewhat dark; then the priest shall shut him up seven days:

22 And if it spread much abroad in the skin, then the priest shall pronounce him unclean: it is a plague.

23 But if the bright spot stay in his place, and spread not, it is a burning boil; and the priest shall pronounce him clean.

24 Or if there be any flesh, in the skin whereof there is a hot burning, and the quick flesh that burneth have a white bright spot, somewhat reddish, or white;

25 Then the priest shall look upon it: and, behold, if the hair in the bright spot be turned white, and it be in sight deeper than the skin; it is a leprosy broken out of the burning: wherefore the priest shall pronounce him unclean: it is the plague of leprosy.

26 But if the priest look on it, and, behold, there be no white hair in the bright spot, and it be no lower than the other skin, but be

somewhat dark; then the priest shall shut him up seven days:

27 And the priest shall look upon him the seventh day: and if it be spread much abroad in the skin, then the priest shall pronounce him unclean: it is the plague of leprosy.

28 And if the bright spot stay in his place, and spread not in the skin, but it be somewhat dark; it is a rising of the burning, and the priest shall pronounce him clean: for it is an inflammation of the burning.

B. On the Head or Beard

Leviticus 13

29 If a man or woman have a plague upon the head or the beard;

30 Then the priest shall see the plague: and, behold, if it be in sight deeper than the skin; and there be in it a yellow thin hair; then the priest shall pronounce him unclean: it is a dry scall, even a leprosy upon the head or beard.

31 And if the priest look on the plague of the scall, and, behold, it be not in sight deeper than the skin, and that there is no black hair in it; then the priest shall shut up him that hath the plague of the scall seven days:

32 And in the seventh day the priest shall look on the plague: and, behold, if the scall

spread not and there be in it no yellow hair, and the scall be not in sight deeper than the skin;

33 He shall be shaven, but the scall shall he not shave; and the priest shall shut up him that hath the scall seven days more:

34 And in the seventh day the priest shall look on the scall: and, behold, if the scall be not spread in the skin, nor be in sight deeper than the skin; then the priest shall pronounce him clean: and he shall wash his clothes, and be clean.

35 But if the scall spread much in the skin after his cleansing;

36 Then the priest shall look on him: and, behold, if the scall be spread in the skin, the priest shall not seek for yellow hair; he is unclean.

37 But if the scall be in his sight at a stay, and that there is black hair grown up therein; the scall is healed, he is clean: and the priest shall pronounce him clean.

38 If a man also or a woman have in the skin of their flesh bright spots, even white bright spots;

39 Then the priest shall look: and, behold, if the bright spots in the skin of their flesh be darkish white; it is a freckled spot that groweth in the skin; he is clean.

40 And the man whose hair is fallen off his head, he is bald; yet is he clean.

41 And he that hath his hair fallen off from the part of his head toward his face, he is forehead bald: yet is he clean.

42 And if mere be in the bald head, or bald forehead, a white reddish sore; it is a leprosy sprung up in his bald head, or his bald forehead.

43 Then the priest shall look upon it: and, behold, if the rising of the sore be white reddish in his bald head, or in his bald forehead, as the leprosy appeareth in the skin of the flesh;

44 He is a leprous man, he is unclean: the priest shall pronounce him utterly unclean; his plague is in his head.

45 And the leper in whom the plague is, his clothes shall be rent, and his head bare, and he shall put a covering upon his upper lip, and shall cry, Unclean, unclean.

46 All the days wherein the plague shall be in him he shall be defiled; he is unclean: he shall dwell alone; without the camp shall his habitation be.

C. In the Garment

Leviticus 13

47 The garment also that the plague of leprosy is in, whether it be a woollen garment, or a linen garment;

48 Whether it be in the warp, or woof; of linen, or of woollen; whether in a skin, or in any thing made of skin;

49 And if the plague be greenish or reddish in the garment, or in the skin, either in the warp, or in the woof, or in any thing of skin; it is a plague of leprosy, and shall be shewed unto the priest:

50 And the priest shall look upon the plague, and shut up it that hath the plague seven days:

51 And he shall look on the plague on the seventh day: if the plague be spread in the garment, either in the warp, or in the woof, or in a skin, or in any work that is made of skin; the plague is a fretting leprosy; it is unclean.

52 He shall therefore burn that garment, whether warp or woof, woollen or in linen, or any thing of skin, wherein the plague is: for it is a fretting leprosy; it shall be burnt in the fire.

53 And if the priest shall look, and, behold, the plague be not spread in the garment, either in the warp, or in the woof, or in any thing of skin;

54 Then the priest shall command that they wash the thing wherein the plague is, and he shall shut it up seven days more:

55 And the priest shall look on the plague, after that it is washed: and, behold, if the plague have not changed his colour, and the plague be not spread; it is unclean; thou shalt burn it in the fire; it is fret inward, whether it be bare within or without.

56 And if the priest look, and, behold, the plague be somewhat dark after the washing of it; then he shall rend it out of the garment, or out of the skin, or out of the warp, or out of the woof:

57 And if it appear still in the garment, either in the warp, or in the woof, or in any thing of skin; it is a spreading plague: thou shalt burn that wherein the plague is with fire.

58 And the garment, either warp, or woof, or whatsoever thing of skin it be, which thou shalt wash, if the plague be departed from them, then it shall be washed the second time, and shall be clean.

59 This is the law of the plague of leprosy in a garment of woollen or linen, either in the warp, or woof, or any thing of skins, to pronounce it clean, or to pronounce it unclean.

D. In the Day of His Cleansing

Leviticus 14

1   And the LORD spake unto Moses, saying,

2   This shall be the law of the leper in the day of his cleansing: He shall be brought unto the priest:

3   And the priest shall go forth out of the camp; and the priest shall look, and, behold, if the plague of leprosy be healed in the leper;

4   Then shall the priest command to take for him that is to be cleansed two birds alive and clean, and cedar wood, and scarlet, and hyssop:

5   And the priest shall command that one of the birds be killed in an earthen vessel over running water:

6   As for the living bird, he shall take it, and the cedar wood, and the scarlet, and the hyssop, and shall dip them and the living bird in the blood of the bird that was killed over the running water:

7   And he shall sprinkle upon him that is to be cleansed from the leprosy seven times, and shall pronounce him clean, and shall let the living bird loose into the open field.

8   And he that is to be cleansed shall wash his clothes, and shave off all his hair, and

wash himself in water, that he may be clean: and after that he shall come into the camp, and shall tarry abroad out of his tent seven days.

9   But it shall be on the seventh day, that he shall shave all his hair off his head and his beard and his eyebrows, even all his hair he shall shave off: and he shall wash his clothes, also he shall wash his flesh in water, and he shall be clean.

10   And on the eighth day he shall take two he lambs without blemish, and one ewe lamb of the first year without blemish, and three tenth deals of fine flour for a meat offering, mingled with oil, and one log of oil.

11   And the priest that maketh him clean shall present the man that is to be made clean, and those things, before the Lord, at the door of the tabemade of the congregation:

12   And the priest shall take one he lamb, and offer him for a trespass offering, and the log of oil, and wave them for a wave offering before the Lord:

13   And he shall slay the lamb in the place where he shall kill the sin offering and the burnt offering, in the holy place: for as the sin offering is the priest's, so is the trespass offering: it is most holy:

14   And the priest shall take some of the blood of the trespass offering, and the priest

shall put it upon the tip of the right ear of him that is to be cleansed, and upon the thumb of his right hand, and upon the great toe of his right foot:

15 And the priest shall take some of the log of oil, and pour it into the palm of his own left hand:

16 And the priest shall dip his right finger in the oil that is in his left hand, and shall sprinkle of the oil with his finger seven times before the LORD:

17 And of the rest of the oil that is in his hand shall the priest put upon the tip of the right ear of him that is to be cleansed, and upon the thumb of his right hand, and upon the great toe of his right foot, upon the blood of the trespass offering:

18 And the remnant of the oil that is in the priest's hand he shall pour upon the head of him that is to be cleansed: and the priest shall make an atonement for him before the LORD.

19 And the priest shall offer the sin offering, and make an atonement for him that is to be cleansed from his uncleanness; and afterward he shall kill the burnt offering:

20 And the priest shall offer the burnt offering and the meat offering upon the altar: and the priest shall make an atonement for him, and he shall be clean.

21 And if he be poor, and cannot get so much; then he shall take one lamb for a trespass offering to be waved, to make an atonement for him, and one tenth deal of fine flour mingled with oil for a meat offering, and a log of oil;

22 And two turtledoves, or two young pigeons, such as he is able to get; and the one shall be a sin offering, and the other a burnt offering.

23 And he shall bring them on the eighth day for his cleansing unto the priest, unto the door of the tabernacle of the congregation, before the LORD.

24 And the priest shall take the lamb of the trespass offering, and the log of oil, and the priest shall wave them for a wave offering before the LORD:

25 And he shall kill the lamb of the trespass offering, and the priest shall take some of the blood of the trespass offering, and put it upon the tip of the right ear of him that is to be cleansed, and upon the thumb of his right hand, and upon the great toe of his right foot:

26 And the priest shall pour of the oil into the palm of his own left hand:

27 And the priest shall sprinkle with his right finger some of the oil that is in his left hand seven times before the LORD:

28 And the priest shall put of the oil that is in his hand upon the tip of the right ear of him that is to be cleansed, and upon the thumb of his right hand, and upon the great toe of his right foot, upon the place of the blood of the trespass offering:

29 And the rest of the oil that is in the priest's hand he shall put upon the head of him that is to be cleansed, to make an atonement for him before the LORD.

30 And he shall offer the one of the turtledoves, or of the young pigeons, such as he can get;

31 Even such as he is able to get, the one for a sin offering, and the other for a burnt offering, with the meat offering: and the priest shall make an atonement for him that is to be cleansed before the LORD.

32 This is the law of him in whom is the plague of leprosy, whose hand is not able to get that which pertaineth to his cleansing.

E. In the House

Leviticus 14

33 And the LORD spake unto Moses and unto Aaron, saying,

34 When ye be come into the land of Canaan, which I give to you for a possession,

and I put the plague of leprosy in a house of the land of your possession;

35 And he that owneth the house shall come and tell the priest, saying, It seemeth to me there is as it were a plague in the house:

36 Then the priest shall command that they empty the house, before the priest go into it to see the plague, that all that is in the house be not made unclean: and afterward the priest shall go in to see the house:

37 And he shall look on the plague, and, behold, the plague be in the walls of the house with hollow strakes, greenish or reddish, which in sight are lower than the wall;

38 Then the priest shall go out of the house to the door of the house, and shut up the house seven days:

39 And the priest shall come again the seventh day, and shall look: and, behold, if the plague be spread in the walls of the house;

40 Then the priest shall command that they take away the stones in which the plague is, and they shall cast them into an unclean place without the city:

41 And he shall cause the house to be scraped within round about, and they shall pour out the dust that they scrape off without the city into an unclean place:

42 And they shall take other stones, and put them in the place of those stones; and he

shall take other morter, and shall plaster the house.

43 And if the plague come again, and break out in the house, after that he hath taken away the stones, and after he hath scraped the house, and after it is plastered;

44 Then the priest shall come and look, and, behold, if the plague be spread in the house, it is a fretting leprosy in the house: it is unclean.

45 And he shall break down the house, the stones of it, and the timber thereof, and all the morter of the house; and he shall carry them forth out of the city into an unclean place.

46 Moreover he that goeth into the house all the while that it is shut up shall be unclean until the even.

47 And he that lieth in the house shall wash his clothes; and he that eateth in the house shall wash his clothes.

48 And if the priest shall come in, and look upon it, and, behold, the plague hath not spread in the house, after the house was plastered: then the priest shall pronounce the house clean, because the plague is healed.

49 And he shall take to cleanse the house two birds, and cedar wood, and scarlet, and hyssop:

50 And he shall kill the one of the birds in an earthen vessel over running water:

51   And he shall take the cedar wood, and the hyssop, and the scarlet, and the living bird, and dip them in the blood of the slain bird, and in the running water, and sprinkle the house seven times:

52   And he shall cleanse the house with the blood of the bird, and with the running water, and with the living bird, and with the cedar wood, and with the hyssop, and with the scarlet:

53   But he shall let go the living bird out of the city into the open fields, and make an atonement for the house: and it shall be clean.

54   This is the law for all manner of plague of leprosy, and scall,

55   And for the leprosy of a garment, and of a house,

56   And for a rising, and for a scab, and for a bright spot:

57   To teach when it is unclean, and when it is clean: this is the law of leprosy.

Chapter 8-Running Issue

A. Out of the Flesh

Leviticus 15
1   And the LORD spake untoMoses and to Aaron, saying,

2   Speak unto the children of Israel, and say unto them, When any man hath a running issue out of his flesh, because of his issue he is unclean.

3   And this shall be his uncleanness in his issue: whether his flesh run with his issue, or his flesh be stopped from his issue, it is his uncleanness.

4   Every bed, whereon he lieth that hath the issue, is unclean: and every thing, whereon he sitteth, shall be unclean.

5   And whosoever toucheth his bed shall wash his clothes, and bathe himself in water, and be unclean until the even.

6   And he that sitteth on any thing whereon he sat that hath the issue shall wash his clothes, and bathe himself in water, and be unclean until the even.

7 And he that toucheth the flesh of him that hath the issue shall wash his clothes, and bathe himself in water, and be unclean until the even.

8 And if he that hath the issue spit upon him that is clean; then he shall wash his clothes, and bathe himself in water, and be unclean until the even.

9 And what saddle soever he rideth upon that hath the issue shall be unclean.

10 And whosoever toucheth any thing that was under him shall be unclean until the even: and he that beareth any of those things shall wash his clothes, and bathe himself in water, and be unclean until the even.

11 And whomsoever he toucheth that hath the issue, and hath not rinsed his hands in water, he shall wash his clothes, and bathe himself in water, and be unclean until the even.

12 And the vessel of earth, that he toucheth which hath the issue, shall be broken: and every vessel of wood shall be rinsed in water.

13 And when he that hath an issue is cleansed of his issue; then he shall number to himself seven days for his cleansing, and wash his clothes, and bathe his flesh in running water, and shall be clean.

14 And on the eighth day he shall take to him two turtledoves, or two young pigeons, and come before the LORD unto the door of the tabernacle of the congregation, and give them unto the priest:

15 And the priest shall offer them, the one for a sin offering, and the other for a burnt offering; and the priest shall make an atonement for him before the LORD for his issue.

Numbers 5
1 And the LORD spake unto Moses, saying

2 Command the children of Israel, that they put out of the camp every leper, and every one that hath an issue, and whosoever is defiled by the dead:

3 Both male and female shall ye put out, without the camp shall ye put them; that they defile not their camps, in the midst whereof I dwell.

4 And the children of Israel did so, and put them out without the camp: as the LORD spake unto Moses, so did the children of Israel.

B. A Man's Seed

Leviticus 15

16 And if any man's seed of copulation go out from him, then he shall wash all his flesh in water, and be unclean until the even.

17 And every garment, and every skin, whereon is the seed of copulation, shall be washed with water, and be unclean until the even.

18 The woman also with whom man shall lie with seed of copulation, they shall both bathe themselves in water, and be unclean until the even.

C. A Woman's issue of Blood

Leviticus 15

19 And if a woman have an issue, and her issue in her flesh be blood, she shall be put apart seven days: and whosoever toucheth her shall be unclean until the even.

20 And every thing that she lieth upon in her separation shall be unclean: every thing also that she sitteth upon shall be unclean.

21 And whosoever toucheth her bed shall wash his clothes, and bathe himself in water, and be unclean until the even.

22 And whosoever toucheth any thing that she sat upon shall wash his clothes, and bathe himself in water, and be unclean until the even.

23 And if it be on her bed, or on any thing whereon she sitteth, when he   toucheth it, he shall be unclean until the even.

24 And if any man lie with her at all, and her flowers be upon him, he shall be unclean seven days; and all the bed whereon he lieth shall be unclean.

25 And if a woman have an issue of her blood many days out of the time of her separation, or if it run beyond the time of her separation; all the days of the issue of her uncleanness shall be as the days of her separation: she shall be unclean.

26 Every bed whereon she lieth all the days of her issue shall be unto her as the bed of her separation: and whatsoever she sitteth upon shall be unclean, as the uncleanness of her separation.

27 And whosoever toucheth those things shall be unclean, and shall wash his clothes, and bathe himself in water, and be unclean until the even.

28 But if she be cleansed of her issue, then she shall number to herself seven   days, and after that she shall be clean.

29 And on the eighth day she shall take unto her two turtles, or two young pigeons, and bring them unto the priest, to the door of the tabernacle of the congregation.

30 And the priest shall offer the one for a sin offering, and the other for a burnt offering; and the priest shall make an atonement for her before the LORD for the issue of her uncleanness.

31 Thus shall ye separate the children of Israel from their uncleanness; that they die not in their uncleanness, when they defile my tabernacle that is among them.

32 This is the law of him that hath an issue, and of him whose seed goeth from him, and is defiled therewith;

33 And of her that is sick of her flowers, and of him that hath an issue, of the man, and of the woman, and of him that lieth with her that is unclean.

Chapter 9-Water of Separation: A Purification for Sin

Numbers 19

1　And the LORD spake unto Moses and unto Aaron, saying,

2　This is the ordinance of the law which the LORD hath commanded, saying, Speak unto the children of Israel, that they bring thee a red heifer without spot, wherein is no blemish, and upon which never came yoke:

3　And ye shall give her unto Eleazar the priest, that he may bring her forth without the camp, and one shall slay her before his face:

4　And Eleazar the priest shall take of her blood with his finger, and sprinkle of her blood directly before the tabernacle of the congregation seven times:

5　And one shall burn the heifer in his sight; her skin, and her flesh, and her blood, with her dung, shall he burn:

6   And the priest shall take cedar wood, and hyssop, and scarlet, and cast it into the midst of the burning of the heifer.

7   Then the priest shall wash his clothes, and he shall bathe his flesh in water, and afterward he shall come into the camp, and the priest shall be unclean until the even.

8   And he that burneth her shall wash his clothes in water, and bathe his flesh in water, and shall be unclean until the even.

9   And a man that is clean shall gather up the ashes of the heifer, and lay them up without the camp in a clean place, and it shall be kept for the congregation of the children of Israel for a water of separation: it is a purification for sin.

10   And he that gathereth the ashes of the heifer shall wash his clothes, and be unclean until the even: and it shall be unto the children of Israel, and unto the stranger that sojourneth among them, for a statute for ever.

11   He that toucheth the dead body of any man shall be unclean seven days.

12   He shall purify himself with it on the third day, and on the seventh day he shall be clean: but if he purify not himself the third day, then the seventh day he shall not be clean.

13   Whosoever toucheth the dead body of any man that is dead, and purifieth not

himself, defileth the tabernacle of the LORD; and that soul shall be cut off from Israel: because the water of separation was not sprinkled upon him, he shall be unclean; his uncleanness is yet upon him.

14 This is the law, when a man dieth in a tent: all that come into the tent, and all that is in the tent, shall be unclean seven days.

15 And every open vessel, which hath no covering bound upon it, is unclean.

16 And whosoever toucheth one that is slain with a sword in the open fields, or a dead body, or a bone of a man, or a grave, shall be unclean seven days.

17 And for an unclean person they shall take of the ashes of the burnt heifer of purification for sin, and running water shall be put thereto in a vessel:

18 And a clean person shall take hyssop, and dip it in the water, and sprinkle it upon the tent, and upon all the vessels, and upon the persons that were there, and upon him that touched a bone, or one slain, or one dead, or a grave:

19 And the clean person shall sprinkle upon the unclean on the third day, and on the seventh day: and on the seventh day he shall purify himself, and wash his clothes, and bathe himself in water, and shall be clean at even.

20 But the man that shall be unclean, and shall not purify himself, that soul shall be cut off from among the congregation, because he hath defiled the sanctuary of the LORD: the water of separation hath not been sprinkled upon him; he is unclean.

21 And it shall be a perpetual statute unto them, that he that sprinkleth the water of separation shall wash his clothes; and he that toucheth the water of separation shall be unclean until even.

22 And whatsoever the unclean person toucheth shall be unclean; and the soul that toucheth it shall be unclean until even.

The Hebrew Israelite Law Book

TITLE 20 – NAZARITE VOW

Numbers 6

1 And the LORD spake unto Moses, saying,

2 Speak unto the children of Israel, and say unto them, When either man or woman shall separate themselves to vow a vow of a Nazarite, to separate themselves unto the LORD:

3 He shall separate himself from wine and strong drink, and shall drink no vinegar of wine, or vinegar of strong drink, neither shall he drink any liquor of grapes, nor eat moist grapes, or dried.

4 AJ1 the days of his separation shall he eat nothing that is made of the vine tree, from the kernels even to the husk.

5 All the days of the vow of his separation there shall no razor come upon his head: until the days be fulfilled, in the which he separateth himself unto the LORD, he shall be holy, and shall let the locks of the hair of his head grow.

6   All the days that he separateth himself unto the LORD he shall come at no dead body.

7   He shall not make himself unclean for his father, or for his mother, for his brother, or for his sister, when they die: because the consecration of his God is upon his head.

8   All the days of his separation he is holy unto the LORD.

9   And if any man die very suddenly by him, and he hath defiled the head of his consecration; then he shall shave his head in the day of his cleansing, on the seventh day shall he shave it.

10   And on the eighth day he shall bring two turtles, or two young pigeons, to the priest, to the door of the tabernacle of the congregation:

11   And the priest shall offer the one for a sin offering, and the other for a burnt offering, and make an atonement for him, for that he sinned by the dead, and shall hallow his head that same day.

12   And he shall consecrate unto the LORD the days of his separation, and shall bring a lamb of the first year for a trespass offering: but the days that were before shall be lost, because his separation was defiled.

13   And this is the law of the Nazarite, when the days of his separation are fulfilled:

he shall be brought unto the door of the tabernacle of the congregation:

14 And he shall offer his offering unto the LORD, one he lamb of the first year without blemish for a burnt offering, and one ewe lamb of the first year without blemish for a sin offering, and one ram without blemish for peace offerings,

15 And a basket of unleavened bread, cakes of fine flour mingled with oil, and wafers of unleavened bread anointed with oil, and their meat offering, and their drink offerings.

16 And the priest shall bring them before the LORD, and shall offer his sin offering, and his burnt offering:

17 And he shall offer the ram for a sacrifice of peace offerings unto the LORD, with the basket of unleavened bread: the priest shall offer also his meat offering, and his drink offering.

18 And the Nazarite shall shave the head of his separation at the door of the tabernacle of the congregation, and shall take the hair of the head of his separation, and put it in the fire which is under the sacrifice of the peace offerings.

19 And the priest shall take the sodden shoulder of the ram, and one unleavened cake out of the basket, and one unleavened wafer,

and shall put them upon the hands of the Nazarite, after the hair of his separation is shaven:

20 And the priest shall wave them for a wave offering before the LORD: this is holy for the priest, with the wave breast and heave shoulder: and after that the Nazarite may drink wine.

21 This is the law of the Nazarite who hath vowed, and of his offering unto the LORD for his separation, beside that that his hand shall get: according to the vow which he vowed, so he must do after the law of his separation.

The Hebrew Israelite Law Book

The Hebrew Israelite Law Book

TITLE 21 – HOLY CONVOCATIONS

Exodus 23

14 Three times thou shalt keep a feast unto me in the year.

15 Thou shalt keep the feast of unleavened bread. (thou shalt eat unleavened bread seven days, as I commanded thee, in the time appointed of the month Abib; for in it thou earnest out from Egypt: and none shall appear before me empty:

16 And the feast of harvest, the firstfruits of thy labours, which thou hast sown in the field: and the feast of ingathering, which is in the end of the year, when thou hast gathered in thy labours out of the field.

Exodus 34

22 And thou shalt observe the feast of weeks, of the first- fruits of wheat harvest, and the feast of ingathering at the year's end.

Leviticus 23

37 These are the feasts of the Lord, which ye shall proclaim to be holy convocations, to offer an offering made by fire unto the Lord, a burnt offering, and a meat offering, a sacrifice, and drink offerings, every thing upon his day:

38 Beside the sabbaths of the LORD, and beside your gifts, and beside all your vows, and beside all your freewill offerings, which ye give unto the LORD.

Chapter 1-Passover 1

Exodus 12

1 AND the LORD spake unto Moses and Aaron in the land of Egypt, saying,

2 This month shall be unto you the beginning of months: it shall be the first month of the year to you.

3 Speak ye unto all the congregation of Israel, saying, In the tenth day of this month

they shall take to them every man a lamb, according to the house of their fathers, a lamb for an house:

4 And if the household be too little for the lamb, let him and his neighbour next unto his house take it according to the number of the souls; every man according to his eating shall make your count for the lamb.

5 Your lamb shall be without blemish, a male of the first year: ye shall take it out from the sheep, or from the goats:

6 And ye shall keep it up until the fourteenth day of the same month: and the whole assembly of the congregation of Israel shall kill it in the evening.

7 And they shall take of the blood, and strike it on the two side posts and on the upper door post of the houses, wherein they shall eat it.

8 And they shall eat the flesh in that night, roast with fire, and unleavened bread; and with bitter herbs they shall eat it.

9 Eat not of it raw, nor sodden at all with water, but roast with fire; his head with his legs, and with the purtenance thereof.

10 And ye shall let nothing of it remain until the morning; and that which remaineth of it until the morning ye shall burn with fire.

11 And thus shall ye eat it; with your loins girded, your shoes on your feet, and your staff

in your hand; and ye shall eat it in haste: it is the LORD'S passover.

12 For I will pass through the land of Egypt this night, and will smite all the firstborn in the land of Egypt, both man and beast; and against all the gods of Egypt I will execute judgment: I am the LORD.

13 And the blood shall be to you for a token upon the houses where ye are: and when I see the blood, I will pass over you, and the plague shall not be upon you to destroy you, when I smite the land of Egypt.

14 And this day shall be unto you for a memorial; and ye shall keep it a feast to the LORD throughout your generations; ye shall keep it a feast by an ordinance for ever.

15 Seven days shall ye eat unleavened bread; even the first day ye shall put away leaven out of your houses: for whosoever eateth leavened bread from the first day until the seventh day, that soul shall be cut off from Israel.

16 And in the first day there shall he an holy convocation, and in the seventh day there shall be an holy convocation to you; no manner of work shall be done in them, save that which every man must eat, that only may be done of you.

Exodus 12

21 Then Moses called for all the elders of Israel, and said unto them, Draw out and take you a lamb according to your families, and kill the passover.

22 And ye shall take a bunch of hyssop, and dip it in the blood that is in the bason, and strike the lintel and the two side posts with the blood that is in the bason; and none of you shall go out at the door of his house until the morning.

23 For the LORD will pass through to smite the Egyptians; and when he seeth the blood upon the lintel, and on the two side posts, the LORD will pass over the door, and will not suffer the destroyer to come in unto your houses to smite you.

24 And ye shall observe this thing for an ordinance to thee and to thy sons for ever.

25 And it shall come to pass, when ye be come to the land which the LORD will give you, according as he hath promised, that ye shall keep this service.

26 And it shall come to pass, when your Children shall say unto you, What mean ye by this service?

27 That ye shall say, It is the sacrifice of the LORD'S passover, who passed over the houses of the children of Israel in Egypt, when he smote the Egyptians, and delivered

our houses. And the people bowed the head and worshipped.

28 And the children of Israel went away, and did as the LORD had commanded Moses and Aaron, so did they.

Leviticus 23

4   These are the feasts of the LORD, even holy convocations, which ye shall proclaim in their seasons.

5   In the fourteenth day of the first month at even is the LORD'S passover.

Chapter 2-Passover 2

Numbers 9

9 And the LORD spake unto Moses, saying,

10 Speak unto the children of Israel, saying, If any man of you or of your posterity shall be unclean by reason of a dead body, or be in a journey afar off, yet he shall keep the passover unto the LORD.

11 The fourteenth day of the second month at even they shall keep it, and eat it with unleavened bread and bitter herbs.

12 They shall leave none of it unto the morning, nor break any bone of it: according to all the ordinances of the passover they shall keep it.

13 But the man that is clean, and is not in a journey, and for- beareth to keep the passover, even the same soul shall be cut off from among his people: because he brought not the offering of the LORD in his appointed season, that man shall bear his sin.

14 And if a stranger shall sojourn among you, and will keep the passover unto the LORD; according to the ordinance of the

passover, and according to the manner thereof, so shall he do: ye shall have one ordinance, both for the stranger, and for him that was born in the land.

Deuteronomy 16

1   Observe the month of Abib, and keep the Passover unto the LORD thy God: for in the month of Abib the LORD thy God brought thee forth out of Egypt by night.

2   Thou shalt therefore sacrifice the passover unto the LORD thy God, of the flock and the herd, in the place which the LORD shall choose to place his name there.

3   Thou shalt eat no leavened bread with it; seven days shalt thou eat unleavened bread therewith, even the bread of affliction; for thou earnest forth out of the land of Egypt in haste: that thou mayest remember the day when thou earnest forth out of the land of Egypt all the days of thy life.

4   And there shall be no leavened bread seen with thee in all thy coast seven days; neither shall there any thing of the flesh, which thou sacrificedst the first day at even, remain all night until the morning.

5   Thou mayest not sacrifice the passover within any of thy gates, which the LORD thy God giveth thee:

6   But at the place which the LORD thy God shall choose to place his name in, there thou shalt sacrifice the passover at even, at the going down of the sun, at the season that thou earnest forth out of Egypt.

7   And thou shalt roast and eat it in the place which the Lord thy God shall choose: and thou shalt turn in the morning, and go unto thy tents.

Chapter 3-Feast of Unleavened Bread

Exodus 12

17 And ye shall observe the feast of unleavened bread; for in this selfsame day have I brought your armies out of the land of Egypt: therefore shall ye observe this day in your generations by an ordinance for ever.

18 In the first month, on the fourteenth day of the month at even, ye shall eat unleavened bread, until the one and twentieth day of the month at even.

19 Seven days shall there be no leaven found in your houses: for whosoever eateth that which is leavened, even that soul shall be cut off from the congregation of Israel, whether he be a stranger, or born in the land.

20 Ye shall eat nothing leavened; in all your habitations shall ye eat unleavened bread.

Exodus 34

1 The feast of unleavened bread shalt thou keep. Seven days thou shalt eat

unleavened bread, as I commanded thee, in the time of the month Abib: for in the month Abib thou earnest out from Egypt.

Leviticus 23

6   And on the fifteenth day of the same month is the feast of unleavened bread unto the LORD : seven days ye must eat unleavened bread.

7   In the first day ye shall have an holy convocation: ye shall do no servile work therein.

8   But ye shall offer an offering made by fire unto the LORD seven days: in the seventh day is an holy convocation: ye shall do no servile work therein.

Numbers 28

16   And in the fourteenth day of the first month is the passover of the LORD.

17   And in the fifteenth day of this month is the feast: seven days shall unleavened bread be eaten.

18   In the first day shall be an holy convocation; ye shall do no manner of servile work therein:

19   But ye shall offer a sacrifice made by fire for a burnt offering unto the LORD; two young bullocks, and one ram, and seven

lambs of the first year: they shall be unto you without blemish:

20 And their meat offering shall be of flour mingled with oil: three tenth deals shall ye offer for a bullock, and two tenth deals for a ram;

21 A several tenth deal shalt thou offer for every lamb, throughout the seven lambs:

22 And one goat for a sin offering, to make an atonement for you.

23 Ye shall offer these beside the burnt offering in the morning, which is for a continual burnt offering.

24 After this manner ye shall offer daily, throughout the seven days, the meat of the sacrifice made by fire, of a sweet savour unto the LORD: it shall be offered beside the continual burnt offering, and his drink offering.

25 And on the seventh day ye shall have an holy convocation; ye shall do no servile work.

Deuteronomy 16
8 Six days thou shalt eat unleavened bread: and on the seventh day shall be a solemn assembly to the Lord thy God: thou shalt do no work therein.

Chapter 4-Sabbath

Exodus 20

8   Remember the sabbath day, to keep it holy.

9   Six days shalt thou labour, and do all thy work:

10   But the seventh day is the sabbath of the LORD thy God: in it thou shalt not do any work, thou, nor thy son, nor thy daughter, thy manservant, nor thy maidservant, nor thy cattle, nor thy stranger that is within thy gates:

11   For in six days the LORD made heaven and earth, the sea, and all that in them is, and rested the seventh day: wherefore the LORD blessed the sabbath day, and hallowed it.

Exodus 23

12   Six days thou shalt do thy work, and on the seventh day thou shalt rest: that thine ox and thine ass may rest, and the son of thy handmaid, and the stranger, may be refreshed.

Exodus 31

12 And the LORD spake unto Moses, saying,

13 Speak thou also unto the children of Israel, saying, Verily my sabbaths ye shall keep: for it is a sign between me and you throughout your generations; that ye may know that I am the LORD that doth sanctify you.

14 Ye shall keep the sabbath therefore; for it is holy unto you: every one that defileth it shall surely be put to death: for whosoever doeth any work therein, that soul shall be cut off from among his people.

15 Six days may work be done; but in the seventh is the sabbath of rest, holy to the LORD: whosoever doeth any work in the sabbath day, he shall surely be put to death.

16 Wherefore the children of Israel shall keep the sabbath, to observe the sabbath throughout their generations, for a perpetual covenant.

17 It is a sign between me and the children of Israel for ever: for in six days the LORD made heaven and earth, and on the seventh day he rested, and was refreshed.

18 And he gave unto Moses, when he had made an end of communing with him upon mount Sinai, two tables of testimony, tables of stone, written with the finger of God.

Exodus 34

21 Six days thou shalt work, but on the seventh day thou shalt rest: in earing time and in harvest thou shalt rest.

Exodus 35

1 And Moses gathered all the congregation of the children of Israel together, and said unto them. These are the words which the LORD hath commanded, that ye should do them.

2 Six days shall work be done, but on the seventh day there shall be to you an holy day, a sabbath of rest to the LORD: whosoever doeth work therein shall be put to death.

3 Ye shall kindle no fire throughout your habitations upon the sabbath day.

Leviticus 19

30 Ye shall keep my sabbaths, and reverence my sanctuary : I am the LORD.

Leviticus 23

1 And the Lord spake unto Moses, saying,

2 Speak unto the children of Israel, and say unto them, Concerning the feasts of the LORD, which ye shall proclaim to be holy convocations, even these are my feasts.

3 Six days shall work be done: but the seventh day is the sabbath of rest, an holy convocation ; ye shall do no work therein: it is the sabbath of the LORD in all your dwellings.

Deuteronomy 5

12 Keep the sabbath day to sanctify it, as the LORD thy God hath commanded thee.

13 Six days thou shalt labour, and do all thy work:

14 But the seventh day is the sabbath of the Lord thy God: in it thou shalt not do any work, thou, nor thy son, nor thy daughter, nor thy manservant, nor thy maidservant, nor thine ox, nor thine ass, nor any of thy cattle, nor thy stranger that is within thy gates; that thy manservant and thy maidservant may rest as well as thou.

15 And remember that thou wast a servant in the land of Egypt, and that the LORD thy God brought thee out thence through a mighty hand and by a stretched out arm: therefore the LORD thy God commanded thee to keep the sabbath day.

Chapter 5-Feast of Harvest

Leviticus 23

9 And the LORD spake unto Moses, saying,

10 Speak unto the children of Israel, and say unto them, When ye be come into the land which I give unto you, and shall reap the harvest thereof, then ye shall bring a sheaf of the firstfruits of your harvest unto the priest:

11 And he shall wave the sheaf before the LORD, to be accepted for you: on the morrow after the sabbath the priest shall wave it.

12 And ye shall offer that day when ye wave the sheaf an he lamb without blemish of the first year for a burnt offering unto the LORD.

13 And the meat offering thereof shall be two tenth deals of fine flour mingled with oil, an offering made by fire unto the LORD for a sweet savour: and the drink offering thereof shall be of wine, the fourth part of an hin.

14 And ye shall eat neither bread, nor parched corn, nor green ears, until the

selfsame day that ye have brought an offering unto your God: it shall be a statute for ever throughout your generations in all your dwellings.

15 And ye shall count unto you from the morrow after the sabbath, from the day that ye brought the sheaf of the wave offering; seven sabbaths shall be complete:

16 Even unto the morrow after the seventh sabbath shall ye number fifty days; and ye shall offer a new meat offering unto the LORD.

17 Ye shall bring out of your habitations two wave loaves of two tenth deals: they shall be of fine flour; they shall be baken with leaven; they are the firstfruits unto the LORD.

18 And ye shall offer with the bread seven lambs without blemish of the first year, and one young bullock, and two rams: they shall be/or a burnt offering unto the LORD, with their meat offering, and their drink offerings, even an offering made by fire, of sweet savour unto the LORD.

19 Then ye shall sacrifice one kid of the goats for a sin offering, and two lambs of the first year for a sacrifice of peace offerings.

20 And the priest shall wave them with the bread of the first- fruits for a wave offering before the LORD, with the two lambs: they shall be holy to the LORD for the priest.

21 And ye shall proclaim on the selfsame day, that it may be an holy convocation unto you: ye shall do no servile work therein: it shall be a statute for ever in all your dwellings throughout your generations.

22 And when ye reap the harvest of your land, thou shalt not make clean riddance of the corners of thy field when thou reapest, neither shalt thou gather any gleaning of thy harvest: thou shalt leave them unto the poor, and to the stranger: I am the LORD your God.

Numbers 28

26 Also in the day of the firstfruits, when ye bring a new meat offering unto the LORD, after your weeks be out, ye shall have an holy convocation; ye shall do no servile work:

27 But ye shall offer the burnt offering for a sweet savour unto the LORD; two young bullocks, one ram, seven lambs of the first year;

28 And their meat offering of flour mingled with oil, three tenth deals unto one bullock, two tenth deals unto one ram,

29 A several tenth deal unto one lamb, throughout the seven lambs;

30 And one kid of the goats, to make an atonement for you.

31 Ye shall offer them beside the continual burnt offering, and his meat offering, (they

shall be unto you without blemish) and their drink offerings.

Deuteronomy 16

9   Seven weeks shalt thou number unto thee: begin to number the seven weeks from such time as thou beginnest to put the sickle to the corn.

10   And thou shalt keep the feast of weeks unto the LORD thy God with a tribute of a freewill offering of thine hand, which thou shalt give unto the LORD thy God, according as the Lord thy God hath blessed thee:

11   And thou shalt rejoice before the Lord thy God, thou, and thy son, and thy daughter, and thy manservant, and thy maidservant, and the Levite that is within thy gates, and the stranger, and the fatherless, and the widow, that are among you, in the place which the Lord thy God hath chosen to place his name there.

12   And thou shalt remember that thou wast a bondman in Egypt: and thou shalt observe and do these statutes.

Chapter 6-Blowing of Trumpets

Leviticus 23

23 And the LORD spake unto Moses, saying,

24 Speak unto the children of Israel, saying, In the seventh month, in the first day of the month, shall ye have a sabbath, a memorial of blowing of trumpets, an holy convocation.

25 Ye shall do no servile work therein: but ye shall offer an offering made by fire unto the LORD.

Numbers 29

1 And in the seventh month, on the first day of the month, ye shall have an holy convocation; ye shall do no servile work: it is a day of blowing the trumpets unto you.

2 And ye shall offer a burnt offering for a sweet savour unto the LORD; one young bullock, one ram, and seven lambs of the first year without blemish:

3   And their meat offering shall be of flour mingled with oil, three tenth deals for a bullock, and two tenth deals for a ram,

4   And one tenth deal for one lamb, throughout the seven lambs:

5   And one kid of the goats for a sin offering, to make an atonement for you:

6   Beside the burnt offering of the month, and his meat offering, and the daily burnt offering, and his meat offering, and their drink offerings, according unto their manner, for a sweet savour, a sacrifice made by fire unto the LORD.

Chapter 7-Day of Atonement

Leviticus 16

1   And the LORD spake unto Moses after the death of the two sons of Aaron, when they offered before the LORD, and died;

2   And the LORD said unto Moses, Speak unto Aaron thy brother, that he come not at all times into the holy place within the vail before the mercy seat, which is upon the ark; that he die not: for I will appear in the cloud upon the mercy seat.

3   Thus shall Aaron come into the holy place: with a young bullock for a sin offering, and a ram for a burnt offering.

4   He shall put on the holy linen coat, and he shall have the linen breeches upon his flesh, and shall be girded with a linen girdle, and with the linen mitre shall he be attired: these are holy garments; therefore shall he wash his flesh in water, and so put them on.

5   And he shall take of the congregation of the children of Israel two kids of the goats for a sin offering, and one ram for a burnt offering.

6   And Aaron shall offer his bullock of the sin offering, which is for himself, and make an atonement for himself, and for his house.

7   And he shall take the two goats, and present them before the LORD at the door of the tabernacle of the congregation.

8   And Aaron shall cast lots upon the two goats; one lot for the LORD, and the other lot for the scapegoat.

9   And Aaron shall bring the goat upon which the LORD's lot fell, and offer him for a sin offering.

10   But the goat, on which the lot fell to be the scapegoat, shall be presented alive before the LORD, to make an atonement with him, and to let him go for a scapegoat into the wilderness.

11   And Aaron shall bring the bullock of the sin offering, which is for himself, and shall make an atonement for himself, and for his house, and shall kill the bullock of the sin offering which is for himself:

12   And he shall take a censer full of burning coals of fire from off the altar before the LORD, and his hands full of sweet incense beaten small, and bring it within the vail:

13   And he shall put the incense upon the fire before the LORD, that the cloud of the incense may cover the mercy seat that is upon the testimony, that he die not:

14   And he shall take of the blood of the bullock, and sprinkle it with his finger upon the mercy seat eastward; and before the mercy seat shall he sprinkle of the blood with his finger seven times.

15 Then shall he kill the goat of the sin offering, that is for the people, and bring his blood within lie vail, and do with that blood as he did with the blood of the bullock, and sprinkle it upon the mercy seat, and before the mercy seat:

16 And he shall make an atonement for the holy place, because of the uncleanness of the children of Israel, and because of their transgressions in all their sins: and so shall he do for the tabernacle of the congregation, that remaineth among them in the midst of their uncleanness.

17 And there shall be no man in the tabernacle of the congregation when he goeth in to make an atonement in the holy place, until he come out, and have made an atonement for himself, and for his household, and for all the congregation of Israel.

18 And he shall go out unto the altar that is before the LORD, and make an atonement for it; and shall take of the blood of the bullock, and of the blood of the goat, and put it upon the horns of the altar round about.

19 And he shall sprinkle of the blood upon it with his finger seven times, and cleanse it, and hallow it from the uncleanness of the children of Israel.

20 And when he hath made an end of reconciling the holy place, and the tabernacle

of the congregation, and the altar, he shall bring the live goat:

21 And Aaron shall lay both his hands upon the head of the live goat, and confess over him all the iniquities of the children of Israel, and all their transgressions in all their sins, putting them upon the head of the goat, and shall send him away by the hand of a fit man into the wilderness:

22 And the goat shall bear upon him all their iniquities unto a land not inhabited: and he shall let go the goat in the wilderness.

23 And Aaron shall come into the tabernacle of the congregation, and shall put off the linen garments, which he put on when he went into the holy place, and shall leave them mere:

24 And he shall wash his flesh with water in the holy place, and put on his garments, and come forth, and offer his burnt offering, and the burnt offering of the people, and make an atonement for himself, and for the people.

25 And the fat of the sin offering shall he burn upon the altar.

26 And he that let go the goat for the scapegoat shall wash his clothes, and bathe his flesh in water, and afterward come into the camp.

27 And the bullock for the sin offering, and the goat for the sin offering, whose blood was brought in to make atonement in the holy place, shall one carry forth without the camp; and they shall burn in the fire their skins, and their flesh, and their dung.

28 And he that burneth them shall wash his clothes, and bathe his flesh in water, and afterward he shall come into the camp.

29 And this shall be a statute for ever unto you: that in the seventh month, on the tenth day of the month, ye shall afflict your souls, and do no work at all, whether it be one of your own country, or a stranger that sojourneth among you:

30 For on that day shall the priest make an atonement for you, to cleanse you, that ye may be clean from all your sins before the LORD.

31 It shall be a sabbath of rest unto you, and ye shall afflict your souls, by a statute for ever.

32 And the priest, whom he shall anoint, and whom he shall consecrate to minister in the priest's office in his father's stead, shall make the atonement, and shall put on the linen clothes, even the holy garments:

33 And he shall make an atonement for the holy sanctuary, and he shall make an atonement for the tabernacle of the

congregation, and for the altar, and he shall make an atonement for the priests, and for all the people of the congregation.

34 And this shall be an everlasting statute unto you, to make an atonement for the children of Israel for all their sins once a year. And he did as the LORD commanded Moses.

Leviticus 23

26 And the LORD spake unto Moses, saying,

27 Also on the tenth day of this seventh month there shall be a day of atonement: it shall be an holy convocation unto you; and ye shall afflict your souls, and offer an offering made by fire unto the LORD.

28 And ye shall do no work in that same day: for it is a day of atonement, to make an atonement for you before the LORD your God.

29 For whatsoever soul it be that shall not be afflicted in that same day, he shall be cut off from among his people.

30 And whatsoever soul it be that doeth any work in that same day, the same soul will I destroy from among his people.

31 Ye shall do no manner of work: it shall be a statute for ever throughout your generations in all your dwellings.

32 It shall be unto you a sabbath of rest, and ye shall afflict your souls: in the ninth day of the month at even, from even unto even, shall ye celebrate your sabbath.

Numbers 29

7   And ye shall have on the tenth day of this seventh month an holy convocation; and ye shall afflict your souls: ye shall not do any work therein:

8   But ye shall offer a burnt offering unto the LORD for a sweet savour; one young bullock, one ram, and seven lambs of the first year; they shall be unto you without blemish:

9   And their meat offering shall be of flour mingled with oil, three tenth deals to a bullock, and two tenth deals to one ram,

10   A several tenth deal for one lamb, throughout the seven lambs:

11   One kid of the goats for a sin offering; beside the sin offering of atonement, and the continual burnt offering, and the meat offering of it, and their drink offerings.

Chapter 8-Feast of Tabernacles

Leviticus 23

34 Speak unto the children of Israel, saying, The fifteenth day of this seventh month shalt be the feast of tabernacles for seven days unto the Lord.

35 On the first day shall be an holy convocation: ye shall do no servile work therein.

36 Seven days ye shall offer an offering made by fire unto the Lord: on the eighth day shall be an holy convocation unto you; and ye shall offer an offering made by fire unto the Lord: it is a solemn assembly; and ye shall do no servile work therein.

Leviticus 23

39 Also in the fifteenth day of the seventh month, when ye

have gathered in the fruit of the land, ye shall keep a feast unto the LORD seven days: on the first day shall be a sabbath, and on the eighth day shall be a sabbath.

40 And ye shall take you on the first day the boughs of goodly trees, branches of palm trees, and the boughs of thick trees, and willows of the brook; and ye shall rejoice before the LORD your God seven days.

41 And ye shall keep it a feast unto the Lord seven days in the year. It shall be a statute for ever in your generations: ye shall celebrate it in the seventh month.

42 Ye shall dwell in booths seven days; all that are Israelites born shall dwell in booths:

43 That your generations may know that I made the children of Israel to dwell in booths, when I brought them out of the land of Egypt: I am the Lord your God.

44 And Moses declared unto the children of Israel the feasts of the LORD.

Numbers 29

12 And on the fifteenth day of the seventh month ye shall have an holy convocation; ye shall do no servile work, and ye shall keep a feast unto the LORD seven days:

13 And ye shall offer a burnt offering, a sacrifice made by fire, of a sweet savour unto the LORD; thirteen young bullocks, two rams, and fourteen lambs of the first year; they shall be without blemish:

14 And their meat offering shall be of flour mingled with oil, three tenth deals unto every

bullock of the thirteen bullocks, two tenth deals to each ram of the two rams,

15 And a several tenth deal to each lamb of the fourteen lambs:

16 And one kid of the goats for a sinemploymen offering; beside the continual burnt offering, his meat offering, and his drink offering.

Numbers 29

17 And on the second day ye shall offer twelve young bullocks, two rams, fourteen lambs of the first year without spot:

18 And their meat offering and their drink offerings for the bullocks, for the rams, and for the lambs, shall be according to their number, after the manner:

19 And one kid of the goats for a sin offering; beside the continual burnt offering, and the meat offering thereof, and their drink offerings.

20 And on the third day eleven bullocks, two rams, fourteen lambs of the first year without blemish;

21 And their meat offering and their drink offerings for the bullocks, for the rams, and for the lambs, shall be according to their number, after the manner:

22 And one goat for a sin offering ; beside the continual burnt offering, and his meat offering, and his drink offering.

23 And on the fourth day ten bullocks, two rams, and fourteen lambs of the first year without blemish:

24 Their meat offering and their drink offerings for the bullocks, for the rams, and for the lambs, shall be according to their number, after the manner:

25 And one kid of the goats for a sin offering; beside the continual burnt offering, his meat offering, and his drink offering.

26 And on the fifth day nine bullocks, two rams, and fourteen lambs of the first year without spot:

27 And their meat offering and their drink offerings for the bullocks, for the rams, and for the lambs, shall be according to their number, after the manner:

28 And one goat for a sin offering; beside the continual burnt offering, and his meat offering, and his drink offering.

29 And on the sixth day eight bullocks, two rams, and fourteen lambs of the first year without blemish:

30 And their meat offering and their drink offerings for the bullocks, for the rams, and for the lambs, shall be according to their number, after the manner:

31 And one goat for a sin offering; beside the continual burnt offering, his meat offering, and his drink offering.

32 And on the seventh day seven bullocks, two rams, and fourteen lambs of the first year without blemish:

33 And their meat offering and their drink offerings for the bullocks, for the rams, and for the lambs, shall be according to their number, after the manner:

34 And one goat for a sin offering; beside the continual burnt offering, his meat offering, and his drink offering.

35 On the eighth day ye shall have a solemn assembly: ye shall do no servile work therein:

36 But ye shall offer a burnt offering, a sacrifice made by fire, of a sweet savour unto the LORD: one bullock, one ram, seven lambs of the first year without blemish:

37 Their meat offering and their drink offerings for the bullock, for the ram, and for the lambs, shall be according to their number, after the manner:

38 And one goat for a sin offering; beside the continual burnt offering, and his meat offering, and his drink offering.

39 These things ye shall do unto the LORD in your set feasts, beside your vows, and your freewill offerings, for your burnt offerings,

and for your meat offerings, and for your drink offerings, and for your peace offerings.

40 And Moses told the Children of Israel according to all that the LORD commanded Moses.

Deuteronomy 16

13 Thou shalt observe the feast of tabernacles seven days, after that thou hast gathered in thy com and thy wine:

14 And thou shalt rejoice in thy feast, thou, and thy son, and thy daughter, and thy manservant, and thy maidservant, and the Levite, the stranger, and the fatherless, and the widow, that are within thy gates.

15 Seven days shalt thou keep a solemn feast unto the LORD thy God in the place which the LORD shall choose: because the LORD thy God shall bless thee in all thine increase, and in all the works of thine hands, therefore thou shalt surely rejoice.

The Hebrew Israelite Law Book

The Hebrew Israelite Law Book

TITLE 22 – MALE APPEARANCE

Exodus 23

17   Three times in the year all thy males shall appear before the Lord GOD.

Exodus 34

23   Thrice in the year shall all your men children appear before the Lord GOD, the God of Israel.

24   For I will cast out the nations before thee, and enlarge thy borders: neither shall any man desire thy land, when thou shalt go up to appear before the LORD thy God thrice in the year.

Deuteronomy 16

16   Three times in a year shall all thy males appear before the LORD thy God in the place which he shall choose; in the feast of unleavened bread, and in the feast of weeks, and in the feast of tabernacles: and they shall not appear before the LORD empty:

17 Every man shall give as he is able, according to the blessing of the Lord thy God which he hath given thee.

TITLE 23 - COMMERCIAL ACTIVITIES

Chapter 1-Weights

Leviticus 19

35 Ye shall do no unrighteousness in judgment, in meteyard, in weight, or in measure.

36 Just balances, just weights, a just ephah, and a just hin, shall ye have: I am the LORD your God, which brought you out of the land of Egypt.

37 Therefore shall ye observe all my statutes, and all my judgments, and do them: I am the LORD.

Deuteronomy 25

13 Thou shalt not have in thy bag divers weights, a great and a small.

14 Thou shalt not have in thine house divers measures, a great and a small.

15 But thou shalt have a perfect and just weight, a perfect and just measure shalt thou have: that thy days may be lengthened in the land which the LORD thy God giveth thee.

16 For all that do such things, and all that do unrighteously, are an abomination unto the LORD thy God.

The Hebrew Israelite Law Book

Chapter 2-Loans

Exodus 22

25 If thou lend money to any of my people that is poor by thee, thou shalt not be to him as an usurer, neither shalt thou lay upon him usury.

Exodus 22

26 If thou at all take thy neighbour's raiment to pledge, thou shalt deliver it unto him by that the sun goeth down:

27 For that is his covering only, it is his raiment for his skin: wherein shall he sleep and it shall come to pass, when he crieth unto me, that I will hear; for I am gracious.

Deuteronomy 23

19 Thou shalt not lend upon usury to thy brother; usury of money, usury of victuals, usury of any thing that is lent upon usury:

20 Unto a stranger thou mayest lend upon usury; but unto thy brother thou shalt not lend upon usury: that the LORD thy God may bless thee in all that thou settest thine hand to in the land whither thou goest to possess it.

Deuteronomy 24

6 No man shall take the nether or the upper millstone to pledge: for he taketh a man's life to pledge.

Deuteronomy 24

10 When thou dost lend thy brother any thing, thou shalt not go into his house to fetch his pledge.

11 Thou shalt stand abroad, and the man to whom thou dost lend shall bring out the pledge abroad unto thee.

12 And if the man be poor, thou shalt not sleep with his pledge:

13 In any case thou shalt deliver him the pledge again when the sun goeth down, that he may sleep in his own raiment, and bless thee: and it shall be righteousness unto thee before the LORD thy God.

Chapter 3-Labor

Exodus 21

2   If thou buy an Hebrew servant, six years he shall serve: and in the seventh he shall go out free for nothing.

3   If he came in by himself, he shall go out by himself: if he were married, then his wife shall go out with him.

4   If his master have given him a wife, and she have born him sons or daughters; the wife and her children shall be her master's, and he shall go out by himself.

5   And if the servant shall plainly say, I love my master, my wife, and my children; I will not go out free:

6   Then his master shall bring him unto the judges; he shall also bring him to the door, or unto the door post; and his master shall bore his ear through with an aul; and he shall serve him for ever.

Exodus 21

20 And if a man smite his servant, or his maid, with a rod, and he die under his hand; he shall be surely punished.

21 Notwithstanding, if he continue a day or two, he shall not be punished: for he is his money.

Leviticus 25

39 And if thy brother that dwelleth by thee be waxen poor, and be sold unto thee; thou shalt not compel him to serve as a bondservant:

40 But as an hired servant, and as a sojourner, he shall be with thee, and shall serve thee unto the year of jubilee:

41 And then shall he depart from thee, both he and his Children with him, and shall return unto his own family, and unto the possession of his fathers shall he return.

42 For they are my servants, which I brought forth out of the land of Egypt: they shall not be sold as bondmen.

43 Thou shalt not rule over him with rigour; but shalt fear thy God.

Leviticus 25

44 Both thy bondmen, and thy bondmaids, which thou shalt have, shall be of the heathen that are round about you; of them shall ye buy bondmen and bondmaids.

45 Moreover of the children of the strangers that do sojourn among you, of them shall ye buy, and of their families that are with

you, which they begat in your land: and they shall be your possession.

46 And ye shall take them as an inheritance for your Children after you, to inherit them for a possession; they shall be your bondmen for ever: but over your brethren the children of Israel, ye shall not rule one over another with rigour.

Leviticus 25

47 And if a sojourner or stranger wax rich by thee, and thy brother that dwelleth by him wax poor, and sell himself unto the stranger or sojourner by thee, or to the stock of the stranger's family:

48 After that he is sold he may be redeemed again; one of his brethren may redeem him:

49 Either his uncle, or his uncle's son, may redeem him, or any that is nigh of kin unto him of his family may redeem him; or if he be able, he may redeem himself.

50 And he shall reckon with him that bought him from the year that he was sold to him unto the year of jubilee: and the price of his sale shall be according unto the number of years, according to the time of an hired servant shall it be with him.

51 If there be yet many years behind, according unto them he shall give again the

price of his redemption out of the money that he was bought for.

52   And if there remain but few years unto the year of jubilee, then he shall count with him, and according unto his years shall he give him again the price of his redemption.

53   And as a yearly hired servant shall he be with him: and the other shall not rule with rigour over him in thy sight.

54   And if he be not redeemed in these years, then he shall go out in the year of jubilee, both he, and his children with him.

55   For unto me the children of Israel are servants; they are my servants whom I brought forth out of the land of Egypt: I am the LORD your God.

Deuteronomy 15

12   And if thy brother, an Hebrew man, or an Hebrew woman, be sold unto thee, and serve thee six years; then in the seventh year thou shalt let him go free from thee.

13   And when thou sendest him out free from thee, thou shalt not let him go away empty:

14   Thou shalt furnish him liberally out of thy flock, and out of thy floor, and out of thy winepress: of that wherewith the LORD thy God hath blessed thee thou shalt give unto him.

15 And thou shalt remember that thou wast a bondman in the land of Egypt, and the LORD thy God redeemed thee: therefore I command thee this thing to day.

16 And it shall be, if he say unto thee, I will not go away from thee; because he loveth thee and thine house, because he is well with thee;

17 Then thou shalt take an aul, and thrust it through his ear unto the door, and he shall be thy servant for ever. And also unto thy maidservant thou shalt do likewise.

18 It shall not seem hard unto thee, when thou sendest him away free from thee; for he hath been worth a double hired servant to thee, in serving thee six years: and the Lord thy God shall bless thee in all that thou doest.

Deuteronomy 23

15 Thou shalt not deliver unto his master the servant which is escaped from his master unto thee:

16 He shall dwell with thee, even among you, in that place which he shall choose in one of thy gates, where it liketh him best: thou shalt not oppress him.

Deuteronomy 24

14 Thou shalt not oppress an hired servant that is poor and needy, whether he be

of thy brethren, or of thy strangers that are in thy land within thy gates:

15   At his day thou shalt give him his hire, neither shall the sun go down upon it; for he is poor, and setteth his heart upon it: lest he cry against thee unto the LORD, and it be sin unto thee.

Chapter 4-Agriculture

Exodus 21

33 And if a man shall open a pit, or if a man shall dig a pit, and not cover it, and an ox or an ass fall therein;

34 The owner of the pit shall make it good, and give money unto the owner of them; and the dead beast shall be his.

Exodus 21

35 And if one man's ox hurt another's, that he die; then they shall sell the live ox, and divide the money of it; and the dead ox also they shall divide.

36 Or if it be known that the ox hath used to push in time past, and his owner hath not kept him in; he shall surely pay ox for ox; and the dead shall be his own.

Exodus 22

29 Thou shalt not delay to offer the first of thy ripe fruits, and of thy liquors: the firstborn of thy sons shalt thou give unto me.

30 Likewise shalt thou do with thine oxen, and with thy sheep: seven days it shall be with his dam; on the eighth day thou shalt give it me.

Exodus 23
10 And six years thou shalt sow thy land, and shalt gather in the fruits thereof:
11 But the seventh *year* thou shalt let it rest and lie still; that the poor of thy people may eat: and what they leave the beasts of the field shall eat. In like manner thou shalt deal with thy vineyard, *and* with thy oliveyard.

Leviticus 19
9 And when ye reap the harvest of your land, thou shalt not wholly reap the corners of thy field, neither shalt thou gather the gleanings of thy harvest.
10 And thou shalt not glean thy vineyard, neither shalt thou gather every grape of thy vineyard; thou shalt leave them for the poor and stranger: I am the Lord your God.

Leviticus 19
19 Ye shall keep my statutes. Thou shalt not let thy cattle gender with a diverse kind: thou shalt not sow thy field with mingled seed: neither shall a garment mingled of linen and woollen come upon thee.

Leviticus 19

23 And when ye shall come into the land, and shall have planted all manner of trees for food, then ye shall count the fruit thereof as uncircumcised: three years shall it be as uncircumcised unto you: it shall not be eaten of.

24 But in the fourth year all the fruit thereof shall be holy to praise the LORD withal.

25 And in the fifth year shall ye eat of the fruit thereof, that it may yield unto you the increase thereof: I am the LORD your God.

Leviticus 25

1 And the LORD spake unto Moses in mount Sinai, saying,

2 Speak unto the children of Israel, and say unto them, When ye come into the land which I give you, then shall the land keep a sabbath unto the LORD.

3 Six years thou shalt sow thy field, and six years thou shalt prime thy vineyard, and gather in the fruit thereof;

4 But in the seventh year shall be a sabbath of rest unto the land, a sabbath for the LORD: thou shalt neither sow thy field, nor prune thy vineyard.

5   That which groweth of its own accord of thy harvest thou shalt not reap, neither gather the grapes of thy vine undressed: for it is a year of rest unto the land.

6   And the sabbath of the land shall be meat for you; for thee, and for thy servant, and for thy maid, and for thy hired servant, and for thy stranger that sojourneth with thee,

7   And for thy cattle, and for the beast that are in thy land, shall all the increase thereof be meat.

Leviticus 25

19 And the land shall yield her fruit, and ye shall eat your fill, and dwell therein in safety.

20 And if ye shall say, What shall we eat the seventh year? behold, we shall not sow, nor gather in our increase:

21 Then I will command my blessing upon you in the sixth year, and it shall bring forth fruit for three years.

22 And ye shall sow the eighth year, and eat yet of old fruit until the ninth year; until her fruits come in ye shall eat of the old store.

Deuteronomy 22

6   If a bird's nest chance to be before thee in the way in any tree, or on the ground,

whether they be young ones, or eggs, and the dam sitting upon the young, or upon the eggs, thou shalt not take the dam with the young:

7   But thou shalt in any wise let the dam go, and take the young to thee; that it may be well with thee, and that thou mayest prolong thy days.

Deuteronomy 22

9   Thou shalt not sow thy vineyard with divers seeds: lest the fruit of thy seed which thou hast sown, and the fruit of thy vineyard, be defiled.

Deuteronomy 22

10   Thou shalt not plow with an ox and an ass together.

Deuteronomy 23

24 When thou comest into thy neighbour's vineyard, then thou mayest eat grapes thy fill at thine own pleasure; but thou shalt not put any in thy vessel.

25 When thou comest into the standing corn of thy neighbour, then thou mayest pluck the ears with thine hand; but thou shalt not move a sickle unto thy neighbour's standing corn.

Deuteronomy 24

19 When thou cuttest down thine harvest in thy field, and hast forgot a sheaf in the field, thou shalt not go again to fetch it: it shall be for the stranger, for the fatherless, and for the widow: that the Lord thy God may bless thee in all the work of thine hands.

20 When thou beatest thine olive tree, thou shalt not go over the boughs again: it shall be for the stranger, for the fatherless, and for the widow.

21 When thou gatherest the grapes of thy vineyard, thou shalt not glean it afterward: it shall be for the stranger, for the fatherless, and for the widow.

22 And thou shalt remember that thou wast a bondman in the land of Egypt: therefore I command thee to do this thing.

Deuteronomy 25
4 Thou shalt not muzzle the ox when he treadeth out the corn.

Chapter 5-The Jubilee

Leviticus 25

8   And thou shalt number seven sabbaths of years unto thee, seven times seven years; and the space of the seven sabbaths of years shall be unto thee forty and nine years.

9   Then shalt thou cause the trumpet of the jubilee to sound on the tenth day of the seventh month, in the day of atonement shall ye make the trumpet sound throughout all your land.

10   And ye shall hallow the fiftieth year, and proclaim liberty throughout all the land unto all the inhabitants thereof: it shall be a jubilee unto you; and ye shall return every man unto his possession, and ye shall return every man unto his family.

11   A jubilee shall that fiftieth year be unto you: ye shall not sow, neither reap that which groweth of itself in it, nor gather the grapes in it of thy vine undressed

12   For it is the jubilee; it shall be holy unto you: ye shall eat the increase thereof out of the field.

13 In the year of this jubilee ye shall return every man unto his possession.

14 And if thou sell ought unto thy neighbour, or buyest ought of thy neighbour's hand, ye shall not oppress one another:

15 According to the number of years after the jubilee thou shalt buy of thy neighbour, and according unto the number of years of the fruits he shall sell unto thee:

16 According to the multitude of years thou shalt increase the price thereof, and according to the fewness of years thou shalt diminish the price of it: for according to the number of the years of the fruits doth he sell unto thee.

17 Ye shall not therefore oppress one another; but thou shalt fear thy God: for I am the LORD your God.

18 Wherefore ye shall do my statutes, and keep my judgments, and do them; and ye shall dwell in the land in safety.

Chapter 6-The Poor

Leviticus 25

25 If thy brother be waxen poor, and hath sold away some of his possession, and if any of his kin come to redeem it, then shall he redeem that which his brother sold.

26 And if the man have none to redeem it, and himself be able to redeem it;

27 Then let him count the years of the sale thereof, and restore the overplus unto the man to whom he sold it; that he may return unto his possession.

28 But if he be not able to restore it to him, then that which is sold shall remain in the hand of him that hath bought it until the year of jubilee: and in the jubilee it shall go out, and he shall return unto his possession.

Leviticus 25

35 And if thy brother be waxen poor, and fallen in decay with thee; then thou shalt relieve him: yea, though he be a stranger, or a sojourner; that he may live with thee.

36 Take thou no usury of him, or increase: but fear thy God; that thy brother may live with thee.

37 Thou shalt not give him thy money upon usury, nor lend him thy victuals for increase.

38 I am the LORD your God, which brought you forth out of the land of Egypt, to give you the land of Canaan, and to be your God.

Deuteronomy 15

7 If there be among you a poor man of one of thy brethren within any of thy gates in thy land which the LORD thy God giveth thee, thou shalt not harden thine heart, nor shut thine hand from thy poor brother:

8 But thou shalt open thine hand wide unto him, and shalt surely lend him sufficient for his need, in that which he wanteth.

9 Beware that there be not a thought in thy wicked heart, saying, The seventh year, the year of release, is at hand; and thine eye be evil against thy poor brother, and thou givest him nought; and he cry unto the LORD against thee, and it be sin unto thee.

10 Thou shalt surely give him, and thine heart shall not be grieved when thou givest unto him: because that for this thing the LORD thy God shall bless thee in all thy

works, and in all that thou puttest thine hand unto.

11 For the poor shall never cease out of the land: therefore I command thee, saying, Thou shalt open thine hand wide unto thy brother, to thy poor, and to thy needy, in thy land.

Chapter 7-Land and Property

Leviticus 25

23 The land shall not be sold for ever: for the land is mine; for ye are strangers and sojourners with me.

24 And in all the land of your possession ye shall grant a redemption for the land.

Leviticus 25

29 And if a man sell a dwelling house in a walled city, then he may redeem it within a whole year after it is sold; within a full year may he redeem it.

30 And if it be not redeemed within the space of a full year, then the house that is in the walled city shall be established for ever to him that bought it throughout his generations: it shall not go out in the jubilee.

31 But the houses of the villages which have no wall round about them shall be counted as the fields of the country: they may be redeemed, and they shall go out in the jubilee.

32 Notwithstanding the cities of the Levites, and the houses of the cities of their possession, may the Levites redeem at any time.

33 And if a man purchase of the Levites, then the house that was sold, and the city of his possession, shall go out in the year of jubilee: for the houses of the cities of the Levites are their possession among the children of Israel.

34 But the field of the suburbs of their cities may not be sold; for it is their perpetual possession.

Numbers 26

52 And the LORD spake unto Moses, saying,

53 Unto these the land shall be divided for an inheritance according to the number of names.

54 To many thou shalt give the more inheritance, and to few thou shalt give the less inheritance: to every one shall his inheritance be given according to those that were numbered of him.

55 Notwithstanding the land shall be divided by lot: according to the names of the tribes of their fathers they shall inherit.

56 According to the lot shall the possession thereof be divided between many and few.

Numbers 34

13 And Moses commanded the children of Israel, saying, This is the land which ye shall inherit by lot, which the LORD commanded to give unto the nine tribes, and to the half tribe:

14 For the tribe of the children of Reuben according to the house of their fathers, and the tribe of the children of Gad according to the house of their fathers, have received their inheritance; and half the tribe of Manasseh have received their inheritance:

15 The two tribes and the half tribe have received their inheritance on this side Jordan near Jericho eastward, toward the sunrising.

Deuteronomy 19

1 When the LORD thy God hath cut off the nations, whose land the LORD thy God giveth thee, and thou succeedest them, and dwellest in their cities, and in their houses;

2 Thou shalt separate three cities for thee in the midst of thy land, which the LORD thy God giveth thee to possess it.

3 Thou shalt prepare thee a way, and divide the coasts of thy land, which the LORD

thy God giveth thee to inherit, into three parts, that every slayer may flee thither.

4 And this is the case of the slayer, which shall flee thither, that he may live: Whoso killeth his neighbour ignorantly, whom he hated not in time past;

5 As when a man goeth into the wood with his neighbour to hew wood, and his hand fetcheth a stroke with the axe to cut down the tree, and the head slippeth from the helve, and lighteth upon his neighbour, that he die; he shall flee unto one of those cities, and live:

6 Lest the avenger of the blood pursue the slayer, while his heart is hot, and overtake him, because the way is long, and slay him; whereas he was not worthy of death, in as much as he hated him not in time past.

7 Wherefore I command thee, saying, Thou shalt separate three cities for thee.

8 And if the LORD thy God enlarge thy coast, as he hath sworn unto thy fathers, and give thee all the land which he promised to give unto thy fathers;

9 If thou shalt keep all these commandments to do them, which I command thee this day, to love the LORD thy God, and to walk ever in his ways; then shalt thou add three cities more for thee, beside these three:

10　That innocent blood be not shed in thy land, which the LORD thy God giveth thee for an inheritance, and so blood be upon thee.

11　But if any man hate his neighbour, and lie in wait for him, and rise up against him, and smite him mortally that he die, and fleeth into one of these cities:

12　Then the elders of his city shall send and fetch him thence, and deliver him into the hand of the avenger of blood, that he may die.

13　Thine eye shall not pity him, but thou shalt put away the guilt of innocent blood from Israel, that it may go well with thee.

Deuteronomy 19

14 Thou shalt not remove thy neighbour's landmark, which they of old time have set in thine inheritance, which thou shalt inherit in the land that the LORD thy God giveth thee to possess it

Chapter 8-Release

Deuteronomy 15

1   At the end of every seven years thou shalt make a release.

2   And this is the manner of the release: Every creditor that lendeth ought unto his neighbour shall release it; he shall not exact it of his neighbour, or of his brother; because it is called the LORD'S release.

3   Of a foreigner thou mayest exact it again: but that which is thine with thy brother thine hand shall release;

4   Save when there shall be no poor among you; for the LORD shall greatly bless thee in the land which the LORD thy God giveth thee for an inheritance to possess it:

5   Only if thou carefully hearken unto the voice of the LORD thy God, to observe to do all these commandments which I command thee this day.

6   For the LORD thy God blesseth thee, as he promised thee: and thou shalt lend unto many nations, but thou shalt not borrow; and thou shalt reign over many nations, but they shall not reign over thee.

The Hebrew Israelite Law Book

TITLE 24 – WARFARE

Exodus 34

10 And he said, Behold, I make a covenant: before all thy people I will do marvels, such as have not been done in all the earth, nor in any nation: and all the people among which thou art shall see the work of the LORD: for it is a terrible thing that I will do with thee.

11 Observe thou that which I command thee this day: behold, I drive out before thee the Amorite, and the Canaanite, and the Hittite, and the Perizzite, and the Hivite, and the Jebusite.

12 Take heed to thyself, lest thou make a covenant with the inhabitants of the land whither thou goest, lest it be for a snare in the midst of thee:

13 But ye shall destroy their altars, break their images, and cut down their groves:

14 For thou shalt worship no other god: for the LORD, whose name is Jealous, is a jealous God:

15 Lest thou make a covenant with the inhabitants of the land, and they go a whoring

after their gods, and do sacrifice unto their gods, and one call thee, and thou eat of his sacrifice;

16 And thou take of their daughters unto thy sons, and their daughters go a whoring after their gods, and make thy sons go a whoring after their gods.

Numbers 31

21 And Eleazar the priest said unto the men of war which went to the battle, This is the ordinance of the law which the LORD commanded Moses;

22 Only the gold, and the silver, the brass, the iron, the tin, and the lead,

23 Every thing that may abide the fire, ye shall make it go through the fire, and it shall be clean: nevertheless it shall be purified with the water of separation: and all that abideth not the fire ye shall make go through the water.

24 And ye shall wash your clothes on the seventh day, and ye shall be clean, and afterward ye shall come into the camp.

Numbers 1

44 These are those that were numbered, which Moses and Aaron numbered, and the princes of Israel, being twelve men: each one was for the house of his fathers.

45 So were all those that were numbered of the children of Israel, by the house of their fathers, from twenty years old and upward, all that were able to go forth to war in Israel

Numbers 31

25 And the LORD spake unto Moses, saying,

26 Take the sum of the prey that was taken, both of man and of beast, thou, and Eleazar the priest, and the chief fathers of the congregation:

27 And divide the prey into two parts; between them that took the war upon them, who went out to battle, and between all the congregation:

28 And levy a tribute unto the LORD of the men of war which went out to battle: one soul of five hundred, both of the persons, and of the beeves, and of the asses, and of the sheep:

29 Take it of their half, and give it unto Eleazar the priest, for an heave offering of the LORD.

30 And of the children of Israel's half, thou shalt take one portion of fifty, of the persons, of the beeves, of the asses, and of the flocks, of all manner of beasts, and give them unto

the Levites, which keep the charge of the tabernacle of the LORD.

31   And Moses and Eleazar the priest did as the LORD commanded Moses.

Deuteronomy 12

1   These are the statutes and judgments, which ye shall

observe to do in the land, which the LORD God of thy fathers giveth thee to possess it, all the days that ye live upon the earth.

2   Ye shall utterly destroy all the places, wherein the nations which ye shall possess served their gods, upon the high mountains, and upon the hills, and under every green tree:

3   And ye shall overthrow their altars, and break their pillars, and burn their groves with fire; and ye shall hew down the graven images of their gods, and destroy the names of them out of that place.

Deuteronomy 20

1   When thou goest out to battle against thine enemies, and seest horses, and chariots, and a people more than thou, be not afraid of them: for the Lord thy God is with thee, which brought thee up out of the land of Egypt.

2   And it shall be, when ye are come nigh unto the battle, that the priest shall approach and speak unto the people,

3   And shall say unto them, Hear, O Israel, ye approach this

day unto battle against your enemies: let not your hearts faint, fear not, and do not tremble, neither be ye terrified because of them;

4   For the Lord your God is he that goeth with you, to fight for you against your enemies, to save you.

5   And the officers shall speak unto the people, saying, What man is there that hath built a new house, and hath not dedicated it? let him go and return to his house, lest he die in the battle, and another man dedicate it.

6   And what man is he that hath planted a vineyard, and hath not yet eaten of it? let him also go and return unto his house, lest he die in the battle, and another man eat of it.

7   And what man is there that hath betrothed a wife, and hath not taken her? let him go and return unto his house, lest he die in the battle, and another man take her.

8   And the officers shall speak further unto the people, and they shall say, What man is there that is fearful and fainthearted? let him go and return unto his house, lest his brethren's heart faint as well as his heart.

9   And it shall be, when the officers have made an end of speaking unto the people, that they shall make captains of the armies to lead the people.

Deuteronomy 20

10 When thou comest nigh unto a city to fight against it, then proclaim peace unto it.

11   And it shall be, if it make thee answer of peace, and open unto thee, then it shall be, that all the people that is found therein shall be tributaries unto thee, and they shall serve thee.

12   And if it will make no peace with thee, but will make war against thee, then thou shalt besiege it:

13   And when the LORD thy God hath delivered it into thine hands, thou shalt smite every male thereof with the edge of the sword:

14   But the women, and the little ones, and the cattle, and all that is in the city, even all the spoil thereof, shalt thou take unto thyself; and thou shalt eat the spoil of thine enemies, which the LORD thy God hath given thee.

15   Thus shalt thou do unto all the cities which are very far off from thee, which are not of the cities of these nations.

16   But of the cities of these people, which the LORD thy God doth give thee for an

inheritance, thou shalt save alive nothing that breatheth:

17 But thou shalt utterly destroy them; namely, the Hittites, and the Amorites, the Canaanites, and the Perizzites, the Hivites, and the Jebusites; as the LORD thy God hath commanded thee:

18 That they teach you not to do after all their abominations, which they have done unto their gods; so should ye sin against the LORD your God.

Deuteronomy 20

19 When thou shalt besiege a city a long time, in making war against it to take it, thou shalt not destroy the trees thereof by forcing an axe against them: for thou mayest eat of them, and thou shalt not cut them down (for the tree of the field is man's life) to employ them in the siege:

20 Only the trees which thou knowest that they be not trees for meat, thou shalt destroy and cut them down; and thou shalt build bulwarks against the city that maketh war with thee, until it be subdued.

Deuteronomy 21

10 When thou goest forth to war against thine enemies, and the LORD thy God hath

delivered them into thine hands, and thou hast taken them captive,

11 And seest among the captives a beautiful woman, and hast a desire unto her, that thou wouldest have her to thy wife;

12 Then thou shalt bring her home to thine house; and she shall shave her head, and pare her nails;

13 And she shall put the raiment of her captivity from off her, and shall remain in thine house, and bewail her father and her mother a full month: and after that thou shalt go in unto her, and be her husband, and she shall be thy wife.

14 And it shall be, if thou have no delight in her, then thou shalt let her go whither she will; but thou shalt not sell her at all for money, thou shalt not make merchandise of her, because thou hast humbled her.

Deuteronomy 23
9 When the host goeth forth against thine enemies, then keep thee from every wicked thing.

10 If there be among you any man, that is not clean by reason of uncleanness that chanceth him by night, then shall he go abroad out of the camp, he shall not come within the camp:

11 But it shall be, when evening cometh on, he shall wash himself with water: and when the sun is down, he shall come into the camp again.

12 Thou shalt have a place also without the camp, whither thou shalt go forth abroad:

13 And thou shalt have a paddle upon thy weapon; and it shall be, when thou wilt ease thyself abroad, thou shalt dig therewith, and shalt turn back and cover that which cometh from thee:

14 For the LORD thy God walketh in the midst of thy camp, to deliver thee, and to give up thine enemies before thee; therefore shall thy camp be holy: that he see no unclean thing in thee, and turn away from thee.

Deuteronomy 25

17 Remember what Amalek did unto thee by the way, when ye were come forth out of Egypt;

18 How he met thee by the way, and smote the hindmost of thee, even all that were feeble behind thee, when thou wast faint and weary; and he feared not God.

19 Therefore it shall be, when the LORD thy God hath given thee rest from all thine enemies round about, in the land which the LORD thy God giveth thee for an inheritance to possess it, that thou shalt blot out the

remembrance of Amalek from under heaven; thou shalt not forget it.

The Hebrew Israelite Law Book

TITLE 25 – ISRAELITE NUMBERING

Exodus 30

11 And the LORD spake unto Moses, saying,

12 When thou takest the sum of the children of Israel after their number, then shall they give every man a ransom for his soul unto the LORD, when thou numberest them; that there be no plague among them, when thou numberest them.

13 This they shall give, every one that passeth among them that are numbered, half a shekel after the shekel of the sanctuary: (a shekel is twenty gerahs:) an half shekel shall be the offering of the Lord.

14 Every one that passeth among them that are numbered, from twenty years old and above, shall give an offering unto the LORD.

15 The rich shall not give more, and the poor shall not give less than half a shekel, when they give an offering unto the LORD, to make an atonement for your souls.

16 And thou shalt take the atonement money of the children of Israel, and shalt appoint it for the service of the tabernacle of the congregation; that it may be a memorial unto the children of Israel before the LORD, to make an atonement for your souls.

Exodus 34
19 All that openeth the matrix is mine; and every firstling among thy cattle, whether ox or sheep, that is male.
20 But the firstling of an ass thou shalt redeem with a lamb: and if thou redeem him not, then shalt thou break his neck. All the firstborn of thy sons thou shalt redeem. And none shall appear before me empty.

Numbers 1
47 But the Levites after the tribe of their fathers were not numbered among them.
48 For the LORD had spoken unto Moses, saying,
49 Only thou shalt not number the tribe of Levi, neither take the sum of them among the children of Israel:
50 But thou shalt appoint the Levites over the tabernacle of testimony, and over all the vessels thereof, and over all things that belong to it: they shall bear the tabernacle, and all the vessels thereof; and they shall

minister unto it, and shall encamp round about the tabernacle.

51 And when the tabernacle setteth forward, the Levites shall take it down: and when the tabernacle is to be pitched, the Levites shall set it up: and the stranger that cometh nigh shall be put to death.

52 And the children of Israel shall pitch their tents, every man by his own camp, and every man by his own standard, throughout their hosts.

53 But the Levites shall pitch round about the tabernacle of testimony, that there be no wrath upon the congregation of the children of Israel: and the Levites shall keep the charge of the tabernacle of testimony.

54 And the children of Israel did according to all that the LORD commanded Moses, so did they.

Numbers 3

11 And the LORD spake unto Moses, saying,

12 And I, behold, I have taken the Levites from among the children of Israel instead of all the firstborn that openeth the matrix among the children of Israel: therefore the Levites shall be mine;

13 Because all the firstborn are mine; for on the day that I smote all the firstborn in the

land of Egypt I hallowed unto me all the firstborn in Israel, both man and beast: mine shall they be: I am the LORD.

14 And the LORD spake unto Moses in the wilderness of Sinai, saying,

15 Number the children of Levi after the house of their fathers, by their families: every male from a month old and upward shalt thou number them.

16 And Moses numbered them according to the word of the LORD, as he was commanded.

Numbers 3

40 And the LORD said unto Moses, Number all the firstborn of the males of the children of Israel from a month old and upward, and take the number of their names.

41 And thou shalt take the Levites for me (I am the LORD) instead of all the firstborn among the children of Israel; and the cattle of the Levites instead of all the firstlings among the cattle of the children of Israel.

Numbers 3

44 And the LORD spake unto Moses, saying,

45 Take the Levites instead of all the firstborn among the children of Israel, and the cattle of the Levites instead of their cattle; and the Levites shall be mine: I am the LORD.

46 And for those that are to be redeemed of the two hundred and threescore and thirteen of the firstborn of the children of Israel, which are more than the Levites;

47 Thou shalt even take five shekels apiece by the poll, after the shekel of the sanctuary shalt thou take them: (the shekel is twenty gerahs:)

48 And thou shalt give the money, wherewith the odd number of them is to be redeemed, unto Aaron and to his sons.

Numbers 4

1   And the LORD spake unto Moses and unto Aaron, saying,

2   Take the sum of the sons of Kohath from among the sons of Levi, after their families, by the house of their fathers,

3   From thirty years old and upward even until fifty years old, all that enter into the host, to do the work in the tabernacle of the congregation.

Deuteronomy 16

19 All the firstling males that come of thy herd and of thy flock thou shalt sanctify unto the LORD thy God: thou shalt do no work with the firstling of thy bullock, nor shear the firstling of thy sheep.

20 Thou shalt eat it before the Lord thy God year by year in the place which the Lord shall choose, thou and thy household.

21   And if there be any blemish therein, as if it be lame, or blind, or have any ill blemish, thou shalt not sacrifice it unto the Lord thy God.

22 Thou shalt eat it within thy gates: the unclean and the clean person shall eat it alike, as the roebuck, and as the hart.

23 Only thou shalt not eat the blood thereof; thou shalt pour it upon the ground as water.

The Hebrew Israelite Law Book

TITLE 26 – SINGULAR VOWS AND SANCTIFYING

Chapter 1-Shekel Payment

Leviticus 27
1   And the LORD spake unto Moses, saying,
2   Speak unto the children of Israel, and say unto them, When a man shall make a singular vow, the persons shall be for the LORD by thy estimation.
3   And thy estimation shall be of the male from twenty years old even unto sixty years old, even thy estimation shall be fifty shekels of silver, after the shekel of the sanctuary.
4   And if it be a female, then thy estimation shall be thirty shekels.
5   And if it be from five years old even unto twenty years old, then thy estimation shall be of the male twenty shekels, and for the female ten shekels.
6   And if it be from a month old even unto five years old, then thy estimation shall be of the male five shekels of silver, and for the female thy estimation shall be three shekels of silver.

7   And if it be from sixty years old and above; if it be a male, then thy estimation shall be fifteen shekels, and for the female ten shekels.

8   But if he be poorer than thy estimation, then he shall present himself before the priest, and the priest shall value him; according to his ability that vowed shall the priest value him.

Chapter 2-Beasts

Leviticus 27

9   And if it be a beast, where of men bring an offering unto the LORD, all that any man giveth of such unto the LORD shall be holy.

10   He shall not alter it, nor change it, a good for a bad, or a bad for a good: and if he shall at all change beast for beast, then it and the exchange thereof shall be holy.

11   And if it be any unclean beast, of which they do not offer a sacrifice unto the Lord,

then he shall present the beast before the priest:

12 And the priest shall value it, whether it be good or bad: as thou valuest it, who art the priest, so shall it be.

13 But if he will at all redeem it, then he shall add a fifth part thereof unto thy estimation.

Leviticus 27

26 Only the firstling of the beasts, which should be the LORD'S firstling, no man shall sanctify it; whether it be ox, or sheep: it is the LORD'S.

27 And if it be of an unclean beast, then he shall redeem it according to thine estimation, and shall add a fifth part of it thereto: or if it be not redeemed, then it shall be sold according to thy estimation.

28 Notwithstanding no devoted thing, that a man shall devote unto the LORD of all that he hath, both of man and beast, and of the field of his possession, shall be sold or redeemed: every devoted thing is most holy unto the LORD.

29 None devoted, which shall be devoted of men, shall be redeemed ; but shall surely be put to death.

Chapter 3-Sanctify His House

Leviticus 27

14 And when a man shall sanctify his house to be holy unto the LORD, then the priest shall estimate it, whether it be good or bad: as the priest shall estimate it, so shall it stand.

15 And if he that sanctified it will redeem his house, then he shall add the fifth part of the money of thy estimation unto it, and it shall be his.

Chapter 4-Sanctifying Fields

Leviticus 27

16 And if a man shall sanctify unto the LORD some part of a field of his possession, then thy estimation shall be according to the seed thereof: an homer of barley seed shall be valued at fifty shekels of silver.

17 If he sanctify his field from the year of jubilee, according to thy estimation it shall stand.

18 But if he sanctify his field after the jubilee, then the priest shall reckon unto him the money according to the years that remain, even unto

the year of the jubilee, and it shall be abated from thy estimation.

19 And if he that sanctified the field will in any wise redeem it, then he shall add the fifth part of the money of thy estimation unto it, and it shall be assured to him.

20 And if he will not redeem the field, or if he have sold the field to another man, it shall not be redeemed any more.

21 But the field, when it goeth out in the jubilee, shall be holy unto the LORD, as a field devoted; the possession thereof Shall be the priest's.

22 And if a man sanctify unto the Lord a field which he hath bought, which is not of the fields of his possession;

23 Then the priest shall reckon unto him the worth of thy estimation, even unto the year of the jubilee: and he shall give thine estimation in that day, as a holy thing unto the LORD.

24 In the year of the jubilee the field shall return unto him of whom it was bought, even to him to whom the possession of the land did belong.

25 And all thy estimations shall be according to the shekel of the sanctuary: twenty gerahs shall be the shekel.

Chapter 5-Men and Women who make a Vow

Numbers 30

1   And Moses spake unto the heads of the tribes concerning the children of Israel, saying, This is the thing which the LORD hath commanded.

2   If a man vow a vow unto the LORD, or swear an oath to bind his soul with a bond; he shall not break his word, he shall do according to all that proceedeth out of his mouth.

3   If a woman also vow a vow unto the LORD, and bind herself by a bond, being in her father's house in her youth;

4   And her father hear her vow, and her bond wherewith she hath bound her soul, and her father shall hold his peace at her: then all her vows shall stand, and every bond wherewith she hath bound her soul shall stand.

5   But if her father disallow her in the day that he heareth; not any of her vows, or of her bonds wherewith she hath bound her soul,

shall stand: and the LORD shall forgive her, because her father disallowed her.

6   And if she had at all an husband, when she vowed, or uttered ought out of her lips, wherewith she bound her soul;

7   And her husband heard it, and held his peace at her in the day that he heard it: then her vows shall stand, and her bonds wherewith she bound her soul shall stand.

8   But if her husband disallowed her on the day that he heard it; then he shall make her vow which she vowed, and that which she uttered with her lips, wherewith she bound her soul, of none effect: and the LORD shall forgive her.

9   But every vow of a widow, and of her that is divorced, wherewith they have bound their souls, shall stand against her.

10   And if she vowed in her husband's house, or bound her soul by a bond with an oath;

11   And her husband heard it, and held his peace at her, and disallowed her not: then all her vows shall stand, and every bond wherewith she bound her soul shall stand.

12   But if her husband hath utterly made them void on the day he heard them; then whatsoever proceeded out of her lips concerning her vows, or concerning the bond of her soul, shall not stand: her husband hath

made them void; and the LORD shall forgive her.

13 Every vow, and every binding oath to afflict the soul, her husband may establish it, or her husband may make it void.

14 But if her husband altogether hold his peace at her from day to day; then he establisheth all her vows, or all her bonds, which are upon her: he confirmeth them, because he held his peace at her in the day that he heard them.

15 But if he shall any ways make them void after that he hath heard them; then he shall bear her iniquity.

16 These are the statutes, which the LORD commanded Moses, between a man and his wife, between the father and his daughter, being yet in her youth in her father's house.

Deuteronomy 23

21 When thou shalt vow a vow unto the LORD thy God, thou shalt not slack to pay it: for the LORD thy God will surely require it of thee; and it would be sin in thee.

22 But if thou shalt forbear to vow, it shall be no sin in thee.

23 That which is gone out of thy lips thou shalt keep and perform; even a freewill offering, according as thou hast vowed unto

the LORD thy God, which thou hast promised with thy mouth.

The Hebrew Israelite Law Book

TITLE 27 - INHERITANCE

Numbers 27

6 And the LORD spake unto Moses, saying,

7 The daughters of Zelophehad speak right: thou shalt surely give them a possession of an inheritance among their father's brethren; and thou shalt cause the inheritance of their father to pass unto them.

8 And thou shalt speak unto the children of Israel, saying, If a man die, and have no son, then ye shall cause his inheritance to pass unto his daughter.

9 And if he have no daughter, then ye shall give his inheritance unto his brethren.

10 And if he have no brethren, then ye shall give his inheritance unto his father's brethren.

11 And if his father have no brethren, then ye shall give his inheritance unto his kinsman that is next to him of his family, and he shall possess it: and it shall be unto the children of

443

Israel a statute of judgment, as the LORD commanded Moses.

Numbers 36

5   And Moses commanded the children of Israel according to the word of the LORD, saying, The tribe of the sons of Joseph hath said well.

6   This is the thing which the LORD doth command concerning the daughters of Zelophehad, saying, Let them marry to whom they think best; only to the family of the tribe of their father shall they marry.

7   So shall not the inheritance of the children of Israel remove from tribe to tribe: for every one of the children of Israel shall keep himself to the inheritance of the tribe of his fathers.

8   And every daughter, that possesseth an inheritance in any tribe of the children of Israel, shall be wife unto one of the family of the tribe of her father, that the children of Israel may enjoy every man the inheritance of his fathers.

9   Neither shall the inheritance remove from one tribe to another tribe; but every one of the tribes of the children of Israel shall keep himself to his own inheritance.

10   Even as the LORD commanded Moses, so did the daughters of Zelophehad:

11 For Mahlah, Tirzah, and Hoglah, and Milcah, and Noah, the daughters of Zelophehad, were married unto their father's brothers' sons:

12 And they were married into the families of the sons of Manasseh the son of Joseph, and their inheritance remained in the tribe of the family of their father.

13 These are the commandments and the judgments, which the LORD commanded by the hand of Moses unto the children of Israel in the plains of Moab by Jordan near Jericho.

Deuteronomy 21

15 If a man have two wives, one beloved, and another hated, and they have born him children, both the beloved and the hated; and if the firstborn son be hers that was hated:

16 Then it shall be, when he maketh his sons to inherit that which he hath, that he may not make the son of the beloved firstborn before the son of the hated, which is indeed the firstborn:

17 But he shall acknowledge the son of the hated for the firstborn, by giving him a double portion of all that he hath: for he is the beginning

of his strength; the right of the firstborn is his.

The Hebrew Israelite Law Book

The Hebrew Israelite Law Book

TITLE 28 – PROPHET

Deuteronomy 18

15 The LORD thy God will raise up unto thee a Prophet from the midst of thee, of thy brethren, like unto me; unto him ye shall hearken;

16 According to all that thou desiredst of the LORD thy God in Horeb in the day of the assembly, saying, Let me not hear again the voice of the LORD my God, neither let me see this great fire any more, that I die not.

17 And the LORD said unto me, They have well spoken that which they have spoken.

18 I will raise them up a Prophet from among their brethren, like unto thee, and will put my words in his mouth; and he shall speak unto them all that I shall command him.

19 And it shall come to pass, that whosoever will not hearken unto my words which he shall speak in my name, I will require it of him.

20 But the prophet, which shall presume to speak a word in my name, which I have not commanded him to speak, or that shall speak

in the name of other gods, even that prophet shall die.

21 And if thou say in thine heart, How shall we know the word which the LORD hath not spoken ?

22 When a prophet speaketh in the name of the LORD, if the thing follow not, nor come to pass, that is the thing which the LORD hath not spoken, but the prophet hath spoken it presumptuously : thou shalt not be afraid of him.

TITLE 29 – ENTERING INTO THE CONGREGATION

Deuteronomy 23

1 He that is wounded in the stones, or hath his privy

member cut off, shall not enter into the congregation of the LORD.

2 A bastard shall not enter into the congregation of the LORD ; even to his tenth generation shall he not enter into the congregation of the LORD.

3 An Ammonite or Moabite shall not enter into the congregation of the LORD; even to their tenth generation shall they not enter into the congregation of the LORD for ever:

4 Because they met you not with bread and with water in the way, when ye came

forth out of Egypt; and because they hired against thee Balaam the son of Beor of Pethor of Mesopotamia, to curse thee.

5　Nevertheless the LORD thy God would not hearken unto Balaam; but the LORD thy God turned the curse into a blessing unto thee, because the LORD thy God loved thee.

6　Thou shalt not seek their peace nor their prosperity all thy days for ever.

7　Thou shalt not abhor an Edomite; for he is thy brother: thou shalt not abhor an Egyptian; because thou wast a stranger in his land.

8　The children that are begotten of them shall enter into the congregation of the LORD in their third generation.

The Hebrew Israelite Law Book

The Hebrew Israelite Law Book

TITLE 30 – CIRCUMCISION

Genesis 17

10 This is my covenant, which ye shall keep, between me and you and thy seed after thee; Every man child among you shall be circumcised.

11 And ye shall circumcise the flesh of your foreskin; and it shall be a token of the covenant betwixt me and you.

12 And he that is eight days old shall be circumcised among you, every man child in your generations, he that is bora in the house, or bought with money of any stranger, which is not of thy seed.

13 He that is born in thy house, and he that is bought with thy money, must needs be circumcised: and my covenant shall be in your flesh for an everlasting covenant.

14 And the uncircumcised man Child whose flesh of his foreskin is not circumcised, that soul shall be cut off from his people; he hath broken my covenant.

Made in the USA
Monee, IL
06 March 2024

54575299R00262